INFINITI

POEMS FROM THE DUGOUT

BY DUGGAN FLANAKIN

"But once in a while
We step outside our reflexes
Recheck our secret indexes
And pause from our role playing
To seek out our own core
And build up our own store,
Our brand, our very special identity."

My challenge to readers of Infinite Galaxies: Poems from the Dugout is that you examine the opportunities in your own lives to invest in the lives of those around you — you will know which ones by the energy you share — and to be prepared for a revolution in your own heart that will translate into new adventures for the soul and body. Love is the answer. It's a great ride!

Dugan

FIRST EDITION

Copyright © 2019 by Duggan Flanakin

PUBLISHED BY:
Duggan's Dugout, PO BOX 81422, Austin, TX 78708-1422
and www.duggansdugout.com
Words by Parch, Austin, TX, USA

ISBN: 978-1-7336003-0-9

COVER ART: Sunny Side Up, by Christina Dietz
The Color Adventurer

PEN AND INK DRAWINGS: Hilary Kuhlmey, Austin-Based Artist

PHOTOGRAPHS: (EXCEPT AS NOTED): Debbie Jayne of Focusography
The Official Duggan's Dugout Photographer

LOGO ART: Nick Thomas-Low, who visited the Dugout during South by Southwest 2013

In loving memory of –

Eluida Hoffpauir Flanakin (1911-2011)

Nancy Dawson Flanakin (1948-2007)

Susan Rebecca Flanakin (1979-2002)

Author's Preface

"That person who helps others simply because it should or must be done, and because it is the right thing to do, is indeed without a doubt, a real superhero." - Stan Lee (2018)

A poem can be defined as a piece of writing that partakes of the nature of both speech and song that is nearly always rhythmical, usually metaphorical ... and arouses strong emotions because of its beauty.

Joyce Kilmer once wrote that, "I think that I shall never see a poem lovely as a tree.... Poems are made by fools like me, but only God can make a tree."

Lovely as trees are, they are nothing compared to humanity, the "crown of creation," made in the image of God, as the story goes. Sadly, most of us fall far short of our potential, which is revealed to us as we follow the lead of the Creator.

The secret to unlocking the "infinite galaxies" within ourselves is to help others "simply because it should or must be done, and because it is the right thing to do." In the process we also discover some of the infinite galaxies often hidden away in the beleaguered hearts of those around us. If we only dare.

It's rather like that image of heaven versus hell as a group of people at a banquet table with long utensils such that the banqueters cannot feed themselves. So the only way to enjoy this paradise is to serve one another. Life is really simple.

Or not. Too many of us are afraid to trust others, and others are so self-absorbed they would never see the obvious. Or they might assume that even if they did feed others, nobody would feed them. So we all starve our hearts together.

Duggan's Dugout was an experiment in creating a community of people who joyfully served one another. It was absolutely essential to my survival that I create such a home, though I hardly saw this at the beginning.

I had lost a beloved daughter, my wife of 30 years, and my mother in a short space of years, and in that order. I was spent. So were my three remaining daughters, only one of whom lived nearby. In choosing who should live in the Dugout, I simply followed the good advice shared by Stan Lee.

What made this community extra special was how we received both strangers (newcomers to the community) and pilgrims (many of whom were traveling musicians) and thereby spread our message of acceptance and caring for one another.

In publishing the poems that came from this period in my life, I felt it necessary to give my readers an overview of my own life and of the life of the Dugout and its "denizens" – both strangers and pilgrims, many of whom have deepened their relationships over the years.

Indeed, this book would not have been possible without this community. Hilary Kuhlmey, whose drawings fill many of these pages, was a frequent visitor who developed her own singing career working with other Dugout denizens.

The quotes on the following page are taken from interviews for a video promoting the Dugout made by denizen Krystina Subieta, a multi-talented electrical engineer, singer, teacher, and music and video producer. On Krysti's first night at a Dugout party, we encouraged her to sing several of her songs, and she has never quit singing to warm our hearts.

Christina Dietz, whose art graces the cover, I met through short-term resident Mark Kelton. Mark was "sent" to the

Denizens Reflect on the Dugout

"I felt like he saw, me, he saw my potential … who I COULD be … to meet someone who saw greatness in me before I could really see it in myself. It was incredible."

Allyssa Milan

"The Dugout is a place where people are able to relax and de-stress and get a foothold on their lives – living here in this community helped save my life."

Debbie Jayne

"Duggan took me in like a son. He doesn't always do things for me that he does for others because he has faith in me. And helping him means a lot to me."

Dion Evans

"The Dugout is an important shelter for people who need second chances. Duggan shows people their value . You notice other people and see their transitions – and think THIS could be ME!"

Jennifer Chilkotowsky

"This is a house where you can be the gamer nerd who wants to hang in your room, the guy who plays the piano in the common area, or those who are just dancing in the living room – all at the same time maybe … it is an awesome space!"

Ethan Alexander

Dugout by Lindsey Wilson, whose first "pilgrimage" was back in 2010. Many of the poems from 2015 came courtesy of denizen Amanda Awethu Blain, who did most of the driving on our journeys that year (as I was recovering from surgery).

Best of all, the Dugout community has over the years become an important part of the lives of my remaining three daughters and of my grandsons. My gratitude for following my heart to open my life to literally hundreds (if not thousands) of strangers and pilgrims provided strong impetus for me – at age 74 – to tell their stories along with sharing my poems.

I finally sold the Dugout house in May 2018, and spent a month here, a few weeks there, until an apartment opened up. Dugout denizen Allyssa Milan was moving to New York, so I sublet her apartment – and began writing those stories.

Of course, it was denizens and friends who moved me into my new dwelling, sustained me with their ongoing friendships, championed my own quest to bring my art to the public, and will surely be my best promoters.

My vision for the foreseeable future is to travel coast to coast and even north to Canada to read my poems and tell my stories, and to collaborate with others whose lives have been touched by this community for the better.

As of now, my dance card is wide open. Hopefully, it will be filling up soon.

Author's Note: Poetry is a forum for contemplation and discussion, not an individual intellectual snack. As such, I urge you to READ THESE POEMS ALOUD. Or at least mouth the words in a suppressed whisper. DISCOVER the poems and feel their energy.

Contents

Duggan and the Dugout

"If loneliness would ever leave my door
I might ne'er have a visitor." --
                    Duggan Flanakin, 1961

Duggan's Dugout evolved from a widower's refuge into a
community house and backyard music venue where I took in
strangers who needed a home, a safe place to grow, mostly after
the storms of life left them shipwrecked … or adrift. People
entered bringing what they had – their energy, their stories,
even their friends. Many of them left strengthened, confident,
and on the path to great success.

The Dugout also took in pilgrims – traveling musicians,
initially those in town for the South by Southwest (SXSW)
Music Festival, Austin's long-running party that keeps
thousands away from the beach during Spring Break. Many of
these musicians would later return over the years, eager to
spend more time with friends who had treated them like family
while on the road.

Duggan's Dugout was the name chosen by its
"denizens" (residents) to the house I had "inherited" after
Nancy, my wife and best friend for 30 years, passed away
following her two-year fight against lung cancer. Young adults
somehow began to trickle into the house in which my beloved
and I had hoped we would grow old together, but which
instead became a memorial to her huge heart.

The poems in this book were all written during my years living
at the Dugout and traveling with Dugout "denizens" (residents
and guests). Emerging from the loss of three of the most
important people in my life, I welcomed the positive energies of

many of these fresh faces and watched other faces turn from negative to positive imagery over their time there.

Unconditional love was the motif at the Dugout. Thus, we daily reinforced the tenet that each human being is created in the image of God and thus is an inheritor of amazing creativity and of priceless inherent value. As we open our eyes, ears, and hearts, a still, small voice will lead us into paths where brass rings abound. Be thankful for the rings you choose to grab.

The Dugout is hardly the only place where people are greeted warmly, hopes and aspirations are shared, and the quest for authenticity is applauded. Everywhere I go I find people with the same hopes, the same awakening to the reality that the authentic life is available and that others will celebrate those who travel up this breath-taking path. As my Chicago friend Meredith Accardi recently put it:

"The people who tried to hold me back only pushed me forward. I began to see my big picture. Life is not about what THEY think. It's about how YOU live. It's about staying true to your dreams, passions, and never stopping . We all have [access to] the Light. Find yours and give it to the ones who want to share in your love light. People of the dark exist, but when you emit universal light, you'll just find a way to shine right through them. Let go and feel the light."

I Started out as a Child

But how did a small-town boy from the Deep South end up as "janitor" and "chauffeur" keeping up with housemates decades younger in trendy Austin, Texas? The story begins a long, long time ago in a village not that far away. My life has been a roller coaster. As a six-year -old, I was a home-run-hitting, fly-catching baseball player in the mold of my hero Ted Williams.

My mother, who later lamented that "the light had gone out of my eyes," never connected her observation to two events that took my soul on a long detour: Being advanced from grade 1 directly to grade 3 (and thus separated from my future Baptist evangelist buddy Wade Akins), and being fitted for eyeglasses at age 8, a condition that turned my line drive home runs all too often into popups or worse.

Sure, I excelled academically, and yes, I played baseball, football, basketball, and tennis with all the other kids – even built forts out of straw (and one year, snow). I even played golf with my father at the small-town country club we enjoyed at a discounted rate. His employer, International Paper Company, had built the course for its (white) employees and their families. An integrated society was hardly even a dream, let alone a reality, for decades to come.

We lived in between bayous and just up the hill from the railroad tracks that northbound led us into south Arkansas in about a ten-minute walk. There were lots of tall trees there to climb. The muddy ditches alongside the railroad tracks also made for great mudbug hunting.

Church was automatic. My mother's mother had died in childbirth, and her dad, valedictorian in his engineering class at Vanderbilt, sent her to Indian Bayou, Louisiana, to live on her Methodist minister grandfather's farm. In the 1930s she worked at a mission school in Dulac, Louisiana, for the Houma Indians, cutting grass and killing snakes to teach English and the Gospel to these Creole speakers who were also part black.

My father's granddad John was the son of John Henry Isaiah Flanakin, a cofounder with Stephen F. Austin of the Texas Colony who returned to rural Louisiana to raise his four children. John Flanakin took a Union bullet in one of the Civil

War's earliest skirmishes in Texas, leaving young John Henry fatherless before his first birthday.

After his mom died seven years later, John Henry was shipped off to Add-Ran Male and Female Christian Academy (a forerunner to Texas Christian University). He became a barber, but his first love was the fiddle. He also raised nine children, of whom my own father was the youngest. Both he and my grandmother, whom he had found while visiting family in Louisiana, lived into their nineties.

You might think I got my love of music from my grandfather, but he was in his eighties when I showed up, retired from his fiddle playing days. He did teach me the art of dominoes and of conversation. He also walked to town every day just to hang out at the local barber shop run by some of his younger cronies.

I was fortunately born in Texas while my dad was stationed at Camp Wolters in Mineral Wells. After being doted on by my parents' army buddies and wives, I was whisked back to the bustling town where my grandparents had chosen to retire (and where two aunts and two older cousins lived).

This was the segregated South. While I had ample choices of which relatives to dine with on a given evening, I was partly raised by the black women my mother hired to watch me while she taught high school English and my dad worked overtime.

My parents had bought nearly an acre of land and built a two-story, four-bedroom house. Later they added a huge family room and breezeway – it was a great party house. To help cover costs, they rented out the two upstairs bedrooms to gentlemen who were in training to help run other paper mills for the company. To four-year-old me, though, they were nice people to visit with. I loved their company ... and their stories.

As a very young white child, my friends and I accepted the local social order as "what it is" and did not see the racism. But in 1952, while recovering from chicken pox and playing bridge with my sainted Aunt Vivian, our radio was tuned to the Republican National Convention. I listened intently as General Eisenhower won the nomination and decided I liked Ike.

In 1955, though, my parents took me to Boston in hopes of seeing the Red Sox play the hated Yankees in a three-game series at Fenway Park. We stayed at the Braemore Hotel and met almost all of the Yankees (my mother's favorite team). She got their autographs (even Yogi Berra), but when we learned that our Jewish friends from dad's army days were not welcome there, we promptly found another place to continue our visit. All three games were rained out, but I learned that racism is personal and hateful and divisive. We are all human.

From then on, it was difficult (though, as a child, I kept quiet, knowing local politics) to sit through silly white people putting on blackface at minstrel shows (didn't Al Jolson do it?). It was even worse to hear respected church people espouse views so directly in contrast to the gospel they claimed to follow. So, naturally, when asked at age 14 by my pastor whether I wanted to be a "preacher," I gave him a horrified look and just said "No." The gospel he was preaching felt hollow, unsatisfying.

Meanwhile, I had survived junior high only to learn that the girl of my dreams was being shipped off to South Carolina with her family. And I was entering high school as an under-aged, socially awkward thirteen-year-old. Worse, my mother, a paragon of virtue for the whole town, was the Student Council sponsor and likely my own English teacher.

On another level, my first year of high school was also the year that my hero President Ike sent troops to enforce *Brown v. Board of Education* in Little Rock. We saw young black children being abused by people who might have been our neighbors. We mostly looked the other way. When the whole community is stuck in the 1870s (where old times are not forgotten, just misremembered), the only way out was one person at a time.

Life got worse. Some unknown physical limitation left me unable to jump off my left foot, so I was off the basketball team. Baseball was no longer a dream, and other sports were just hobbies engaged in with one's neighbors. I became a sports writer, and that got me a job with the local weekly. Then one day, it all came crashing down.

My social awkwardness reared its ugly head, and I got suspended from school for losing my temper. I lost my job with the local paper, so I turned back to hanging out at the radio station. Music was my escape – and my energy.

In my senior year I was the driver-host to our Sicilian foreign exchange student, Pietro. I also was chosen to attend a state high school leadership conference. One of the guys there announced he could always tell a Jew based on some stupid claim. I challenged him to pick out which of his three companions was Jewish. His face turned red, as he realized his ignorance. He apologized to all three of us and became an advocate against anti-Semitism. He too had learned that we are all the same – humans seeking our own destiny.

I had offers from lots of colleges. I mean, I was a National Merit Finalist with a 1420 SAT score (and a year younger than most others taking the test). But I was a football fan, so I went to Louisiana State, following my dad, two uncles, and an aunt who became my college guidance counselor.

One day a friend from San Antonio claimed her dad had built his dental office using money paid by then-Senator Lyndon Johnson, whom he had allegedly caught illegally slant-well drilling under his property. Who knows? But I had gained contempt for the man who would soon be President.

I worked in vain to elect Charlton Lyons, Louisiana's first serious Republican candidate for Governor since Reconstruction. The guy who won was a racist. I worked alongside Morton Blackwell, who became the founder of the small-government activist training group Leadership Institute.

The Intersection of Faith and Politics

I will never forget the chaos at the student union that fateful morning in November 1963, nor the quick decision by my bud Charles McBride to hop on a plane and report on the saddest funeral of our time. Burying John Fitzgerald Kennedy marked the end of our innocence. It also put the "despicable" Lyndon Johnson in the White House.

I had spent the previous summer in Washington, DC, attending summer school and rooming with future U.S. Senator Larry Pressler (and meeting Doris Kearns before she became LBJ's biographer). Civil rights marches and demonstrations were the rage. I was seeing how life was lived outside Louisiana. That experience, plus my aunt and uncle living in Silver Spring, led me back to Washington after I graduated college in 1965.

My Republicanism of the day was heavily influenced by the seeming motto of the Louisiana Democratic establishment that public office was a license to steal. What a contrast to the teaching in our civics classes that public officials are elected to serve the people. It never occurred to me that a corrupt people will surely have corrupt leaders.

Of course, it was easy to oppose "Lyndon Johnson's war." Though I had a government job (as a science editor), I was quickly recruited into Students for a Democratic Society. Not long after, I started assisting the fledgling Washington *Free Press,* using my journalist skills to help with layout, printing, and distribution, and later writing news articles, even the paper's writeup of Arlo Guthrie's first Washington concert.

We always had music at our anti-war rallies, and so I quickly got into the local music scene. Billy Danoff (who cowrote 14 songs with John Denver, including "Take Me Home Country Roads") and his wife Taffy Nivert had a band called Fat City; Chris and Susan Sarandon were among their backup vocalists. Later, as the Starland Vocal Band, they had another bit hit, "Afternoon Delight."

Other friends included Claude Jones, the first American to be arrested for possessing LSD, and Bob Berberich, Paul Dowell, and other guys who helped introduce future E Street Band guitarist Nils Lofgren to the music world. The highlight musically was the "First Human Be-In" concert at P Street Beach in Washington, DC. But my greatest honor was getting to work with the light show (connected to the paper) for four nights of Jimi Hendrix. After that week, I was "experienced."

Working with the *Free Press* and Liberation News Service (at our shared Thomas Circle offices) led me to a one-time sharing of "doobies" with Abbie Hoffman and Jerry Rubin. More frequent hangouts were with Black Panthers, stone hippies, New Agers, and all manner of characters, including my eclectic group of roommates. We celebrated, during a concert with The Who, as we learned LBJ was not running for reelection.

The year 1968 was horrific. We cried in April when the Rev. Dr. Martin Luther King, Jr., was murdered, brought baskets of food and clothing to our inner-city friends after riots broke out a month later, then cried again in June when Bobby Kennedy was gunned down. Then Clean Gene McCarthy (the antiwar candidate) lost the Democratic nomination to Hubert Humphrey in the aftermath of the Days of Rage in Chicago. Even many in the New Left voted for Nixon. But really, there was no choice: Both were war hawks.

By early 1969 the war had gone from bad to worse, as our anti-war coalition had shattered. My Yippie friends at Liberation News Service had split from the hard-liner New Leftists at the *Free Press.* In early June, at a gathering at Cathy Wilkerson's Adams Morgan home, she, together with Bernadine Dohrn, Bill Ayers, and Kathy Boudin, challenged us to join with them in the violent Weathermen. I had earlier expressed my views as Bernadine's escort to her speech at Georgetown University by giving her a balloon, urging her to "lighten up."

By this time, though, I had dropped totally out of my job, seeking for the first time to find my own identity. It was a wild time. *The Whole Earth Catalog* (a Sears catalog for the counter culture) was out, and there were hippie stores opening all over.

On the first day of June, I moved into "Morrison Hotel" with Paul Martin Smith (who would later work as a film editor on such movies as "Star Wars: Episode I"), Mary Jo Myers (whose grandparents founded *Highlights for Children*), and other roommates – and a parade of short-termers and visitors.

The following year I rented a second house with different hippie friends, including draft resister Robert Adams, affectionately known within the "movement" as "Wonder Warthog." We cooked macrobiotic food; I worked for a time as a pot washer at a fancy country club. We still saw ourselves as hippies, revolutionaries. Yet, little by little our utopian dream was falling apart.

Shortly afterward, I wrote these words in a letter to my mother:

Why do idealists have to be beaten, condemned, and jailed? Or run over by a limousine? If people won't listen to pleas, entreaties, cries, burnings, manifestos, boycotts, they're just going to have to listen to obscenities, watch their children shoot heroin and have breakdowns, see their businesses and homes burned, and so forth. It's hard to shrug off frustration when you're fighting for freedoms that matter -- I mean, nobody cares if they get hosed down at a panty raid.

In early 1971, I rented a flat in Adams Morgan but gave it up to fly out to San Francisco with friends. My next stop was my parents' home in Louisiana. I promptly got a job at the paper mill and bought a VW microbus.

I was desperately seeking a meaningful life, learning to ride horses on my much older cousin's ranch. Then he keeled over and died while mowing his yard, and I was totally lost. The previous spring, I had met a woman in Washington who was now miserably dealing with severe allergies and languishing at her parents' home outside Miami. I drove that bus all the way down and back (with her and six parrots and her five-year-old daughter). In March 1972 we got married in my parents' home in "a fever" and what must have been guilt.

Then we drove back to Washington, got an apartment for a minute. Then she learned she was pregnant and wanted to go home. But as soon as we arrived in Miami, I was sent packing. Two months later, I found a house to share with some friends that was near the Potomac River in Cabin John, Maryland. Devastated at my total life failure, I really began soul searching.

One day visitors from Wisconsin invited me to a 10-mile hike the C & O Canal pathway from Great Falls, Maryland, back to our house (a block from the canal). The next day I walked along the canal from the house to M Street – another several miles. My old friend Wayne Rodgers (aka Turkey), former road manager for the Jefferson Airplane and well-known hippie leader. He said he was on his way to a Bible study.

His life changes intrigued me, so I went to his house two days later. That night, he convinced me to stop striving and put my trust in God. As soon as I got back home that same night, I got the call that my daughter Payton was born.

After a failed attempt at reconciliation (back in Miami), I spent two years crying and cleansing my anguished soul. We hippie Christians (so-called) hungered and thirsted so much that we went from church to church to worship service to Bible study. One day we were being taught by a female Assemblies of God minister, the next by two young lay Catholic Charismatics, the next by the white pastor of a nearly all-black congregation.

We were awed as Africans led services where the power of the Holy Spirit was on display, and humbled as we worshipped with Messianic Jews. In the churches we frequented, race and color were no longer relevant at all. (Or so we thought.)

I also found an abandoned house, talked the owners into letting me live there in exchange for fixing it up. I moved in a couple of friends (one visually impaired) and lived there for years rent-free in return for replacing all the broken windows, ripping out the busted drywall, adding insulation, then new drywall and new paint. We also developed a sizable garden.

Faith, Hope, and True Love

By this time, I was driving the "Bicentennial Yellow Cab" – my 1976 Ford vehicle painted red, white, and blue – and gaining some notoriety and some contempt. One Sunday I saw the face of an angel in the church balcony, and the next day I met the great love of my life, my wife and partner Nancy Dawson. My

single days were again soon over. We had a huge church
wedding 75 days later. I adopted her two-year-old daughter
Genevieve, and we quickly produced Susan and Melody.

I had gotten my old job back as a government science editor,
worked on the side with *Progressive Vision,* a newspaper that
supported Judeo-Christian Restoration Ministries. The founder,
Tom Hess, had a vision for bringing Christian pastors and other
spiritual leaders together to put aside their differences and pray
to a common God for healing of the lands. We hosted huge
conferences with such Christian leaders as South Korea's Paul
Yonggi Cho, pastor of the world's largest Christian
congregation, and Senate Chaplain Richard Halverson of
Washington's Fourth Presbyterian Church.

Three of my pals convinced me to be the voice of a weekly
music radio program, "Branches," which featured
"Washington's Christian Music Makers." Our program also
sponsored a contest, with about 70 entrants, with the winner
getting to perform on the main stage at a nearby music festival.

Somehow, I talked myself into a partnership to transform an
old biker bar in College Park, Maryland, into "The SonShine
Inn." The idea was a combination ice cream bar and restaurant
with live (Christian) music – even the famous Randy Stonehill
played our venue. Problem was too many cooks – each partner
had a different vision. The place closed six months after
opening, but after I had sold my interest to the other partners.

Meanwhile, Nancy and I had bought an old six-bedroom house
in College Park and begun taking in strangers and pilgrims.
One was a new mother Nancy had counseled at a crisis
pregnancy center. Carmen Louise taught our children to eat
Mexican food, especially after Nancy "pole-vaulted" down the
basement stairs, banged her head, and was laid up for three
months. We had weekly community gatherings and hosted

traveling troubadours, as well as our singer-songwriter pastor Brian McLaren, who later become a best-selling Christian author and leader.

In the fall of 1986, my zeal for truth and adventure led us to pursue a graduate degree in public policy at Regent University in Virginia Beach. One of my college jobs was working to elect Mark Earley, who later became Virginia's Attorney General, as a state senator, largely because he won labor union support. Our children thrived in the academic environment.

Times got harder, though, when we moved to Louisiana after my classroom time was over. I eventually got a job writing about environmental regulations and their impact on local governments, businesses, and individuals. Nancy got a grant that helped pay for her Master's in Library and Information Science. Fast forward to 1994, when I was named a Senior Fellow with Texas Public Policy Foundation and we moved to a Houston suburb.

Finally, as Nancy would say it, I began to get the help I needed to overcome my lifelong bouts with uncontrolled "blackout" anger. The answer was simple. I just had to believe that I COULD maintain control. [I had a long history of putting fists through doors and walls, and of yelling that stemmed from childhood punishments interrupted by parental arguments over the nature and extent of my punishment.]

We went through tough economic times in Houston, yet still managed to find an alternative school for my youngest daughter and three of her closest friends (all with absentee fathers) who came to live at our house. I had to start all over as owner and publisher (not just hired-hand writer) of the regulatory newsletter that was paying our bills at a time when increasing internet presence made that newsletter less valuable.

Baptized into the Austin Music Scene

When Nancy and I moved to Austin in 1999, I had no idea I would be working hand in hand with some of Austin's best musicians, including some of Austin's best teenaged musicians. Nor did either of us know that she would create a domestic and sexual violence library now housed at the University of Texas.

On Easter Sunday, the final day of South by Southwest (SXSW) 2000, we stopped into the venerable reggae bar and Jamaican food haven Shaggy's, which was, sadly, shutting down the next day. On this day, Shaggy's hosted the Imperial Golden Crown Harmonizers. This super group, put together by well-known musicians like Gurf Morlix and Papa Mali (Malcolm Welbourne), sang gospel songs to raise money for local charities. Other than lunch, they took nothing for themselves for two hours of joyful music that kept us going.

Perhaps it was the impassioned vocals of E. R. Shorts, perhaps it was just the recognition that these players were being true servants. A week later, Nancy and I found ourselves at the Empanada Parlor, where a young Damon Lange was running sound for the Harmonizers and getting his Nomad Sound business off the ground. And I was passing the collection plate and lugging gear in and out to help the band's mission.

Not long after, we met Greg Adkins, who had been making records of gospel music performed by the Harmonizers and other prominent musicians in the area. Through Greg we built relationships with Malford Milligan (of the band Storyville), country-bluegrass singer Brennen Leigh (and her brother Seth Hulbert), and others who worked with Greg's project.

We also frequented the Hole in the Wall bar near the University of Texas campus to catch shows with the band

Quatropaw and activist songwriter Steve Ulrich, who was our daughter Susan's favorite. In the process strait-laced "No Nonsense Nellie" (the name Nancy had used for the advice column she wrote for "Neighbors" in Baton Rouge) and I entwined ourselves with all the members of the hippie groups the South Austin Gospel Choir and Body Choir.

We had been commissioned at our local church, along with evangelist-songwriters Rocky Ivy and (later) James Bruce, to reach out to the Austin music community. These were the "radical" Christians, yet their rote approach to "evangelism" (rather than simple love) failed to engage the creatives they sought to enlist. Perhaps they had assumed their "mission" gave them teacher status. But these highly skilled musicians wanted to participate, not be sung to by amateurs.

So Nancy and I went rogue. Instead of asking people to come meet us on our turf, we went in faith to theirs. Our experience had taught us that love must be given and received with no strings, not even "church attendance." Deeds, not words, are what change futures. And Nancy and I made many real friends who stuck with us during the hard times that were to come.

Any doubt that Nancy and I were making a difference should have been resolved after Susan's tragic death in May 2002. First, Greg Adkins, James Bruce, and that community held us together through the funeral and relocation to a new house. All of us were in shock; we were just going through the motions.

Then, to our surprise, we got a call from Jason Richard of Quatropaw offering a special seder in Susan's honor at their home. There, Jason and his songwriter-florist wife Beth, eventual best-selling author Jackson Michael, social instigator Amanda Winters, noted sculptor and Renaissance Woman Cheryl Latimer, and Susan's favorite Steve Ulrich showed us a love that exceeded our wildest expectations. We spent six hours in prayer being encouraged by these "nontraditional" lovers of God (who knew how to love their fellow humans).

Shortly afterward, many of these friends spent another six hours with us at Susan's memorial service. Dozens of Susan's friends drove up from Houston to honor her life and her spirit – a spirit that inspires me even today. Jackson played all six hours. Both experiences gave us new strength to move forward. Now it was our turn to pass that love on to others as we lived through our grief.

Things were still tough for us when we had a second blow. An unlicensed driver, spooked by a state cop, pulled his girlfriend's grandparents' unregistered vehicle directly in front of us and I just "knew" we were dead. Our car was totaled, I had a broken ankle. Nancy had serious contusions from her life-saving seat belt. It took months for us to recover.

A few months later, to help us through our grief and our recovery, some from that seder encouraged me to begin writing the Flanfire music blog. Staying home (after we recovered from our injuries) was hard, so we went out most nights to hear mostly local bands. And I was an experienced music writer.

This service to the music community opened doors for me that I had never expected. Nancy's great love had enveloped me enough that even I was gladly received in this alternate reality community. Things got even richer when Nancy and I began going out to listen to teenage bands, a tradition later continued with my 97-year-young mother.

In January 2005, we finally bought our dream home. Our young next-door neighbor promised us as soon as we saw the back yard, we would know this was where we belonged. One look at the live oak trees and we were sold. That year was wonderful – good friends, good times. But in early December, Nancy knew she was ill again.

This time it was lung cancer (she was never a smoker), stage 4. She could not even climb the stairs to our bedroom during months of chemo. Meanwhile, my mother's acumen was failing, and so we decided to get a second (one-story) house nearby to accommodate both of my invalid angels.

The market was going south, and we did not find a buyer for our dream home. We sublet to musicians like our old friend Bryce Clifford and Phil Brown, who years earlier had replaced the late Lowell George as singer and guitarist for the legendary rock band Little Feat. Phil brought rock legend Mark Andes (Heart, Spirit, Firefall), my old friend Malford Milligan (Storyville), and rock legend Pat Mastelotto (King Crimson, Mr. Mister, XTC) to the house to rehearse their short-lived project M2P2. Perhaps the energy they left behind helped fuel the musical energy at the Dugout.

When we learned that Nancy had contracted meningitis and was surely going to leave us, musician friends poured into her hospital room even as she was in a coma and sang songs to her for hours. When she was transferred to hospice, she awoke and was very present for the next four days, where again she was surrounded by music with friends and unseen angels, and, yes, hundreds of butterfly kisses. Chad Pope and Wendy Colonna even drove 400 miles to sing to her one last time.

Nancy's memorial service was "limited" to three hours, and Austin music icon Nancy Coplin kept the 18 musical groups and 15 personal testimonies flowing. I recall saying something about us all having scars invisible to the naked eye but not to the caring soul.

Still, I had my mother, and I kept in shape pushing her around in her wheelchair to all manner of music events. I was helping Gretchen Barber (immortalized in a ZZ Top song) book talent for Romeo's, a now-defunct Austin restaurant. One of my mother's biggest thrills was dining with me at Romeo's, meeting the performing musicians, and clapping and singing along to their tunes.

On another occasion, I took her to a teen rock show featuring a young Jake Lauterstein. Turns out Jake's grandma and my mother were old friends who got to revisit old times and smile at being "grandma groupies." What a surprise!

Once Nancy's estate was settled, I thought to use some of the proceeds to upgrade our old "dream house" to sell it. But as the work was being done, I felt a strong call to move back in. Only years later did I realize that I had been called back to finish the work that Nancy and I might have done together (now that our own children were out on their own).

Blues Mafia, Blastbeat, and The O'My's

Even when she was sick, Nancy was almost as frequent a music flyer as I. It was she who really made my work meaningful with her great ability to chat one on one. I will always remember how she encouraged our friend Jackson in his writing. The article he wrote for a newspaper I worked for briefly was never published, but still he pursued his dream.

A few years later Jackson interviewed 40 National Football League legends, then wrote *The Game before the Money: Voices of the Men Who Built the NFL*, a book that opened new doors. He parlayed that success into a radio show and a documentary film, *We Were the Oilers: The Luv Ya Blue Era*. Maybe Nancy's encouragement was what set this shy hippie guitarist who "barely finished high school" on his own rise to prominence.

In 2006, some of our music friends, led by Natalie Zoe and her not-yet-18-year-old daughter Sasha Ortiz, threw a benefit concert that enabled me to stay home and give my wife the best care a man could give a woman with stage 4 lung cancer. Later that year, Sasha (who would later sing backup for Sharon Jones and the Dap Kings), joined a teen band called Blues Mafia, together with bassist Kai Roach, drummer Chris Copeland, guitarist and singer Max Frost (now an international touring artist), and second guitarist Patrick Mertens.

It was through our working with those then-teenagers and their families that I met Irish music maven Robert Stephenson. Through this connection I was introduced to emerging talented musicians from across the United States – and beyond. After "retiring" from big-show booking, Robert had founded Blastbeat, a program that uses music concerts as a medium for teaching business management techniques to teenagers,. He started in Ireland and later expanded worldwide.

In 2008, Blastbeat hosted a day party during the South by Southwest (SXSW) Music Festival and invited Blues Mafia to perform. I ran to the venue, then invited Robert, Ryan Sweeney, and the rest of the Blastbeat team to see another Austin teen band (the fledgling Mother Falcon). Then I asked how I could help their work. Later that year, Blastbeat Austin was born, expanding quickly to half a dozen local high schools. Blues Mafia won the Austin competition, earning them a trip to Dublin, Ireland, to perform at the Blastbeat World Finals.

Early in 2009, Ryan Sweeney called me from Chicago with a problem. The Irish economy had soured, and Blastbeat's primary sponsor had bailed. Ryan, however, wanted to bring the local contest winners to play the scheduled Blastbeat showcase in Austin.

To help make their dreams come true, I offered to put up three teenagers from The O'My's in my house. I also found the band a local horn section and got them extra gigs that showed Austin that these kids could play. Little did I know what was being set in motion. Blues Mafia had laid the foundation, but The O'My's were the ones who tapped into the potential, sent their friends my way, and welcomed me into their homes as well.

Today, singer-guitarist Maceo Haymes and keyboardist Nick Hennessey remain the core of the band. Bassist Carter Lang performed at the Grammys in 2018 as bassist and producer for five-time nominee SZA. Drummer Michael Piolet won a full scholarship to the jazz program at the University of Miami. Rapper Zack Wicks remains a Chicago legend years after a heart attack took his life before his twenty-third birthday. I miss this loving brother every day.

The Birth of the Dugout

The ongoing legend of the Dugout began during South by Southwest the following year. Had March 2010 not happened, the events of March 2009 might have quickly faded away. In February 2010, Maceo from The O'My's called me up to explain that the band was not coming to SXSW that year.

The real reason for his call, though, was to introduce me to Lindsey Wilson, who at age 22 was hosting a ten-band day party showcase for Chicago bands. Could I help her out, Maceo asked? He explained that she had just raised a second five thousand dollars to pay for the showcase after the record label which was to co-sponsor the showcase had backed out at the last minute. I said, I will see what I can do.

Next thing I knew, Sonny White and others from the band Ouachita helped me build a stage in between two gorgeous live oak trees in the Dugout backyard. Sonny worked at Home

Depot, so I got his discount on the lumber. We learned that our stage was legal, because the next-door neighbor called the cops to try to shut our party down. Cops came, measured the stage, said all was well. We just had to limit the party to fifty people at a time and keep the sound at 70 decibels maximum.

No one should have bothered. All week long the weather was sunny and in the seventies. Several of the Chicago bands docked first at the Dugout, including Lindsey's band The Down Feathers, Kellen (Kirwan) and Me, a Chicago band actually called "How Far to Austin," and Teddy Grossman and the soulful Great Divide. We woke up Saturday morning to 33-degree temperatures and 30-mile-per-hour wind gusts.

Relieved at confrontation avoidance, we quietly moved the party indoors. No one complained. Not even when the St. Louis band Brothers Lazaroff tore the roof off the house with their combination of soul, spirit, and psychedelic sounds. We had Children of the Feather, The Down Feathers, Box of Baby Birds, and Lauren Bruno and PolySky. We had Mohawk-wearing Brett Randell and long-haired Chicago hippie Remington Pettygrove. It was a glorious time.

And then it happened. The five minutes that changed my life forever. My old Blastbeat buddy Ryan Sweeney had secretly been gathering verses from his Chicago pals (and from my six-year-old grandson Caleb) for a big finale. Ryan first sang us one of his own compositions, and I suspected NOTHING.

Little did I know that Chicago photographer Michael Litchfield had set up a camera as his mates gathered on stage (along with Austin's Scott Evans on fiddle) to sing six verses of a song they dubbed, "Dear Duggan." The foot stomping began, and Kellen announced, "This song goes out to Duggan." Next, I heard the chorus, "Dear Duggan ... we'd like to say, 'thank you.'"

Left to Right: Michael Litchfield, Caleb Cornelius, Kellen Kirwan, Ryan Sweeney (guitar), Brett Randell (mohawk), and Lindsey Wilson.

Litchfield led off, then Lindsey, then her bandmate Jarryd Steimer, then Scott. Caleb began his verse, then started giggling. Kellen admitted he never got around to writing his verse, so Ryan finished up. But the music rolled on, with more hand claps, a piano, and finally Ryan helped Caleb sing his verse, which included, "You're the best grandpa I know."

I was floored. And only then did Michael tell me he had recorded the event for posterity. [The live version can be found at www.duggansdugout.com.] Years later, another Dugout denizen, Krysti Subieta, would make a short video commemorating the final few years of the Dugout.

But love works in more than one direction. Two months later I was sleeping on a couch at the house Maceo and Nick shared in Chicago's Wicker Park (Sarah Cowles, who was assisting at my job and living at the Dugout, was next door with Nick's parents). I was living in their world: inner city meets intellectual, activist Chicago. I had arrived.

In the next year alone I made three more trips to Chicago, always staying with "the boys," each time being more integrated into the Chicago music community. Lindsey Wilson introduced me to her Michigan friend Maren Celest (who now performs with the world-renowned shadow puppeteers Manual Cinema) at a loft party with six bands, rope dancing, and more.

Maceo and Nick brought me into the Chicago hiphop scene and their pals Ice Face, NoName, Malcolm London, and Chancellor Bennett (Chance the Rapper). Michael Johnson

Dancing with Audiotree's Nikki Hartel.

and Adam Thurston of Audiotree Records, now owners of music venues Schuba's and Lincoln Hall, welcomed me as a brother. In 2013 I brought my dancing shoes to their debut Audiotree Music Festival in Kalamazoo (see photo, page 23).

The Dugout Goes Nationwide

The unexpected outpouring of love through song from these new Chicago friends guaranteed that I would always open my home to traveling soldiers using music with love as their weapon of choice. In the years that followed, I produced many SXSW shows and day parties – and other benefit concerts and parties as well. Nearly everything that happened here was an act of love and serendipity as one random act of kindness led to another and another and another.

In 2011, Great Divide and the Down Feathers returned to play, along with 33 other acts, at a three-day "SX620 festival" at a Mexican restaurant known for its sunsets. I partnered with Clifton Axtell and Dugout denizen Victoria Johnson, and with restaurant manager Kevin Harney, another old friend, to get audio and video recordings of each performance.

Meanwhile, I had booked traveling bands I knew at several other venues, and again housed several travelers. Chicago-based Midwest Hype played a stirring set at 11 pm on Saturday night after their van broke down near Mobile, Alabama. They had driven all day and night in a rental van just to play their one SXSW gig.

While visiting Chicago in October 2011, I was Audiotree's guest at a live audio and video taping for the Brooklyn-based band Rubblebucket. Upon learning that their first national tour was bringing them to Austin on a cold Sunday night in November, I persuaded the promoters to add Holiday, a popular local band, to the bill.

Rubblebucket, building on those new friendships, has returned to Austin many times, most recently as headliners at Utopia Fest 2018. Holiday's bassist, Wayne Dalchau, is one of the principal creators of that ten-year-old festival. Wayne has also recruited me to perform in several music videos, including a Wild Child video in which I am mowing a yard with a push mower wearing a Speedo.

In 2012, The O'My's returned, along with Paper Thick Walls, a band Ryan Sweeney was promoting. Another Dugout visitor, Judson McKinney, called on his way from Los Angeles to ask if he could stay at the house and bring "a friend" with him. "A friend" turned into 22 southern Californians from

From left to right: Bridgette Seasons, Maceo Haymes, John Seasons, Duggan Flanakin, and Nick Hennessey reunited in October 2018. Haunted Summer and The O'My's had time to scarf some barbecue and revisit 2012.

three bands, many of whom camped in the backyard and sang (and swam late at night) in the creek across the street.

Also that year, Victoria Johnson and I co-hosted a day party at the nearby Nomad Bar. The O'My's headlined an afternoon of rap and hiphop that featured The Illphonics from St. Louis (who likewise have become good friends over the years) plus rap groups from Houston, Austin, and Madison, Wisconsin.

The Duggan's Dugout logo is from the 2013 visitors who all signed a huge card made of a large sheet of poster paper. Bassist-artist Nick Thomas-Low painted a representation of my face on the front quarter. That year, I booked well over 120 slots for performers at seven different venues during the week. I had long since learned that the key to musicians' hearts is to provide them with an audience and maybe a stage.

In 2014 longtime friend Kole Hansen was working with blogger Ryan Spaulding and Counting Crows frontman Adam Duritz on their "Outlaw Roadshow." She called, asking if I could help a Portland band, Acoustic Minds, which had just missed the cut for their Austin SXSW showcase. We have booked them every year since, and Austin is now their second home.

We threw our annual party that year on a Sunday. That morning I had gotten a call from Vivi McConnell. We had met in 2011 when we invited her brother's band Santah to close out our SX620 party on Lake Travis. Vivi's band Grandkids had a show canceled, and could they drive in and stay the night? Sure, I said – but be ready to play the party. And so they did.

Grandkids was on tour with Cold Fronts from Philadelphia, who arrived the next day. Both bands practiced at the Dugout. We also had one-time Austin teenage sensation Alex Campbell and his jazz-rock band from Berklee School of Music, and a host of other denizens plus Kyle Evans of Echo Bloom, whom we had met two days earlier at the Outlaw Roadshow.

In 2015 The O'My's were back at the Dugout, joined by Denver bands MegaGem (a sweet family band) and Tyto Alba, fronted by tattoo artist Melanie Steinway. I had met Kris Jackson of the band I Am Love who was in Austin framing art for my friend Landry McMeans. He contacted old band mate Joshua Christopher, who was at the time living in Denver.

Joshua also invited Dani Mari, a Philly ex-pat living in Brooklyn (and creator of the Brookadelphia music coop). I had known about Dani and had separately invited her, but he brought her. She too has become a trusted friend who shares a house in Brooklyn with longtime Dugout denizen Allyssa Milan (whose Austin apartment I sublet when she moved).

That same year Al Smith from Cold Fronts returned to host a Philadelphia day party at one of the clubs we hosted shows. We also got a call from our friend Merri Palmer that Captain Squeegee, a band from Phoenix which had toured with her friend's band from Amarillo, was touring through Austin with the Canadian trio Redrick Sultan (from Vancouver). Trumpet player-singer Danny Torgersen has become a close friend, returning multiple times with Squeegee, his other Phoenix band Fayuca, and with the Sublime tribute band Badfish.

The highlight of the 2016 day party was the twilight set by Chicago's Bassel and the Supernaturals. Bassel Almadani is a Syrian-American bandleader and friend of How Far to Austin's Derrick Mitchell, who had referred Bassel's band to me.

In one of my visits to Chicago, I had introduced Derrick to Maggie Mitchell, as they were both Mitchells (of different colors and genders) and both experienced singers of the National Anthem. Their friendship has led to an anthem duet, multiple theater performances, and doubtless lots of food and fun. Why NOT introduce your friends to others whose company they might enjoy to their mutual benefit?

The 2017 day party began at noon outside on a beautiful day with Grace Park of the San Marcos-based touring band The Deer leading with a solo set. One of the highlights was CALICO, a country band from Los Angeles featuring 2012 Dugout veteran Kaitlin Wolfberg (now strings director for southern California's Wild Honey Orchestra) on fiddle.

This party also marked the Dugout debut of guitarist Ryan Koronich, who had just moved to Austin from Fort Collins, Colorado. He walked in with guitar in hand, and we immediately called him up to the stage, to be joined by members of The Holy Child (transplants from Downey, California, who had moved to Austin and performed regularly at the Dugout) and Palestinian-American rapper-jazz singer Abuzayed the Free. Our mutual friend, guitar legend Phil Brown, had been called away from his set and we needed a sub.

The 2018 Dugout Day Party – the final one at the house that became home for dozens over the years – may have been the best. Many bands and solo performers had long histories with the Dugout, including John and Bridgette Seasons of Haunted Summer (who as members of different bands had fallen in love at the Dugout during SXSW 2012), Brett Randell (who had helped paint the living room back in January 2010), and Craig Almquist and Cold Fronts (from Philadelphia).

We closed out with two last-minute invitees -- La Fonda from Seattle and Beams from Toronto -- whom one of our number had met earlier in the week. The next week the house went up on the market, and two months later the Dugout house had become a part of our history.

What I Learned about Love and Life

There was so much joy, despite some rough moments, at the Dugout. Still, I knew that one day I would be encouraged to move on – to finally grow up enough to "leave the Dugout" (the nest). Maybe that's why I wrote the first of many poems about leaving the Dugout behind four years before we finally packed up and moved forward.

Looking back (briefly), I realize that, after a decade of living with the hope of tomorrow, instead of growing older, I had grown (much) younger again. I had gained much, and built the framework for new projects, new adventures, new friends to share life with during each of each year's three hundred sixty-five suns. And yet there are so many more stories -- enough to fill at least one more book (or more). And there are story tellers from the Dugout who may soon be telling some of them.

These poems, all written between 2012 and 2018 and presented in chronological order, reflect the encouragement I received and the friendships I have enjoyed from opening my empty home to an ever-changing ragtag group of strangers and pilgrims who like me were desperately seeking their own future. The heart I received that empowered and commissioned me to welcome those "sent" my way was surely the broken heart of my beloved daughter Susan, who had left this sweet old world far too soon. She would have felt right at home there.

These poems tell my story of thriving after great loss by taking my friend Natalie Zoe's advice and pouring my energies into the lives of others at a very personal level. In my travels I have been a guest at my friends' sold-out theater shows in Chicago and other cities, and I have felt the funereal sadness of losing close (young) friends to violence and pain. I have stayed up past sunrise many times taking in the late-night air and deep bonding and sharing secret thoughts and fears – and triumphs.

These poems also tell the stories of my companions, and of some we encountered along the way. The old house is under new management, but the Dugout of the heart is thriving and growing in adherents to our recognition that each human soul is a treasure house of great value that oftentimes needs to be unlocked for us – and the soul – to comprehend.

Former denizens are sharing the values they lived out at the Dugout into their own new spaces. I see seeds planted years ago now as tall trees ripening to maturity and full of fruit. Everywhere I find Dugout-connected friends espousing our philosophy of loving more, judging less. As frequent Dugout visitor Becca Kadison posted recently, *"I will not stand idly by and live in a world where unconditional love is invisible…. Find your own way to swing the pendulum in the direction of love."*

This book is thus a testament to the concept of sharing what you have with those who have a need and a thirst for life. The Dugout met my own need to create a new story for the rest of my life. The sharing and caring spirit our community provided has been life-changing for so many. It is their stories – in their own words -- I hope to share in forthcoming posts on the Dugout website and perhaps in a future book.

One more thing I have learned is to never limit your future. When I first decided to finally publish this book of poems, I had no idea that I would be asked to recite them in public. Now I am being called upon to expand my conversations with people to the broader issues of how to live a fulfilling life based on my own experiences. I think had I known I might have been tempted for a moment to shoot myself in the foot again.

I mean, yes, I had won third place in a statewide high school extemporaneous speaking competition, but I well remember shaking like a leaf and not having a clue as to what I had spoken to my audience of fellow contestants and judges. Writing poems was something I could do in private – not exposing my true self to the world I feared would mock me.

But now – at seventy-four years young -- I feel compelled to go into the world, visiting friends old and new. I want to share these poems and the message that we grow when we open our hearts to strangers and pilgrims, when we unburden ourselves of our excessive stuff and listen to our hearts to find ways to maximize the impact of our charity . We should also recognize that our largesse is also indicative of our need for community.

My poems often spill out of my heart and head in a stream of consciousness. It is often as if I am transcribing words I have received rather than invented or created myself. I am thankful especially to Jeff and David Lazaroff for their song "Lament," in which Jeff reminds us that paying attention costs us nothing but often yields *"huge jackpots … you can cash in wherever and whenever in so many various ways."*

So we listen to the voice of the Universe – but we then have to step forward and act on what we are hearing. Thus, the guy who never thought he would write a book or publish his poems is willing to stand up and face audiences as a poet in my eighth decade. Who says you cannot teach an old dog new tricks?

Except, of course, in many ways I am still a young pup about to embark on his first solo tour. If you like the poems in this book, I encourage you to bring me to your community.

I urge you as you read these poems to seek your own love light. Know that this light operates by the principle of giving and receiving. Give first, and God (or the universe, if you prefer), who has your best interests at heart, will supply you with the tools for a joyful, fulfilling life that is uniquely yours.

Dugout Pilgrims Weighing In

"The love you share makes this world a better place. Thank you for all you do."

Lindsey Wilson and Jarryd Steimer (2010)

"Duggan – You must be some kind of guardian angel. I am so very grateful that you came into our lives. Your kindness, generosity and sagacity are the stuff of legends. Thank you for everything."

Kate White (2013)

"Thank you so much for everything. We never would have made it down here without you.:"

Josh Werblun (2013)

"Thank you SO much!!! Your help was amazing. Thank you for the kindness, the hospitality, and the great time. You are one of a kind!"

Rogelio, Eric, Mauricio, and Jonah from Los Angeles (friends of friends, 2015)

"Thanks for everything you did for us. That was one of the best experiences we've ever had."

Chad Gosselin, The Big Lonesome (2017)

The Poems

I have been writing poems for a long time. Here's an excerpt from one I wrote in 1974, entitled "Back on Your Feet."

Getting back on your feet
After walking in your brother's shoes
Is a relief
And you pick up speed
Work a little bit and earn his respect
And know
That you'll never be the same again ….

And here is another from the same year:

I was told when a child
How not to be a child
And so became a man … dying.

Whereupon I felt my soul
(or was it my Spirit?)
And was (re)born(e) …
A new self, crystal clear,
With the old encased within
For only me to see
(or so I thought)
And upon my first seeing
I sought to put on new clothes
(for I was ashamed) …

The first poem in the Dugout series, written on New Year's Day 2011, sets the tone for the poems in this series. What if, instead of following our "leaders" and dividing ourselves into factions, we instead decided just to "go out and love someone you were taught to hate" and to "find common ground."

The New Year
January 1, 2011

A pox on the new year
I didn't will it
But it is there …
Debt
Greed
Egomania
And, of course, the desire to be gods

But there is hope
That the leveling will come
Not as the kings and queens demand, but
When we realize we are one yet not the same.

When we stop look and listen
To the rulers of the game
Our hope springs eternal
Yet we fall back down, afraid

But hope fulfilled requires
That we seize the day
Not fade away
Into nothingness

Hope fulfills itself through love
And so
The only way to beat the system
Is to declare it irrelevant
And love those deemed unworthy
By those who are in the know.

Worry, doubt, and fear kill hope
They divide and conquer
So to be free we must
Break down barriers
Make friends with those least likely
Find common ground

Ignore, no, defy the labels
They create.
Don't hesitate!
Go out and love someone
You were taught to hate
Or even worse, despise demean
Defrock Dehumanize Destroy

One day we will survive
Solely because we have loved
The unlovely,
And they, the ruling class,
The trend setters,
The holier thans
Will find themselves
At the mercy of hobos.

Note: I first shared this poem after the House Wine open mic with Christopher Rains, Judson McKinney, Mary Silvergirl, and others who set the poem to dirge-like music and showed me just how I might present my poems in a public setting. Thus, this is the perfect poem to begin this collection.

Cardboard Cutouts
September 20, 2012

Length and height but no depth
And no time
Images of humanoids who pass through our lives
Like ships in the night
Meaningless interruptions of our solitude.

Shadow people with no story to tell
That's the way we see them.
We sense their presence
But take no stock of their humanity
No time to discover the many treasures
That lie within their hidden hearts.

Seven billion souls
But we
Can only meld
With one or two or three or four or none
The rest
We hardly see
Because we care not or dare not be real in turn.

Once in a while
We encounter
Ourselves.
Are we too made of cardboard?
Easily burned in the fires of life,
Easily thrown into the recycle bin,
Easily discarded, discounted, distant, dry?

O are we warm and real and moving through life
At the speed of heartache?
Can others feel us, breathe with us
Cry with us, laugh with us?
Do we have context?

Dare we breathe deeply to let life in?
Dare we open our souls in space and time
Dare we see that
Those we once passed by
Once saw as cardboard cutouts
Once easily ignored
Are calling out
See me Feel me Touch me Heal me
Just as we in our muted voices
Want to believe our own lives have meaning.

NOTE: A special thanks to filmmaker and friend Jeffrey Travis and to his film "Flatland."

Done
July 18, 2014

Done
Well, almost.
Wrapping packages
Sorting through books, records, stuff.

About time to fly
A new adventure
Leaving the ferry behind
Where to go
How long the journey

Unknown
Unimportant
Each day matters
And yet
The end
Is of little consequence.

What does count
Is setting things right
Not to disrupt the lives
Of those to be left ahead
Because they are not behind
The times.
They have their own tomorrows
And you
Have no yesterdays.

Today
Is eternal
Is vital
Is honorable to pursue
Leaving a legacy
Of discovery.

Being
A mellow yellow fellow
Who hears the symphony
And knows the notes to play
And when to be silent.

The song goes on
Even if the player
Is no more
To be found

Because the right notes
Lead to the next verse
And the chorus
Will be sung
As a living eulogy
Years after
Your bones have ceased to be.

But who knows
How long
Or how far and wide
Your ship will sail
Before it disappears
Into the ocean of Neverland.

Meanwhile
Each today
Is special
Fabulous
Ethereal
And history making.

Stories
December 22, 2014

We all have our stories
And our story …
And yet
Who will listen?
Who indeed will tell their own?

I mean, you hear a lotta bravado
You hear a lot of good times ending bad
You hear a little truth mixed in with the lies
That we tell to ensure our status
Our hang
Our gang
Us.

But none of "us" really listen to real stories
That are too tough to handle
Without getting a little bit burned
Or confronted
With our own reality --
And who wants that?

And yet we have to be as children
Not faking adulthood
Or even pretending to be tough,
Or even mean,
To be ready for real stories,
Our tales of memories, mementoes,
And photographs
From long ago

"Why do you keep these ?"
Is almost never asked.

Who really wants to know
How you caught the game ball
How you climbed over a person's wall

And found a treasured friend
On the other side?

On my wall I have stories.
Lisa and Sophie came to town
Met an angel who showed them how to love
Now they are both moms
Way up in Canada.
And I too have a note
That keeps me anchored
To the reality of my own frailty.

And a lease
That reminds me
I once was a child prince
Living in a wicked kingdom
And yet imagining heroes
Lived all around me.
Knights in tarnished armor,
A princess waiting for her chariot
Which turned out to be a motorcycle,
And Hollywood's real children
Warts and all.

But who wants to hear those stories?
Is truth really stranger than fiction?
Is life even true?

Our stories we know
And our story
We are learning as we go
But if a story falls in the forest
And no one hears
Did it even matter?

The Dead Don't Have Girlfriends
(or do they?)

January 11, 2015

I want a girlfriend
I said to my boss.
But you're dead, he reminded me.
But I don't feel dead, I replied.

That's because you walk among the living
More alive than they are
Because you chose to die.
And now you want to live as they do
Though dead you breathe rarefied air.
Have you lost your mind?
Have you lost heart?

Be careful what you wish for,
As you only see
The tip of the iceberg
The world in two, maybe three dimensions.

I see through time
I know your needs
And what you need
You have in spades
And I know how it feels to be lonely
I know how it feels to be betrayed.

I know how it feels
To let life go
Or rather its illusion
To end the confusion
And stop the intrusion

Of a poisonous infusion
Of the elixir
The pseudo fixer
That kills the spirit
And chills the soul.

Instead, be whole.
Be bold.
Live your death
To its fullest
And you never know
What surprises may unfold.

I wanted to respond
To point out that
Laundry, dishes, taxes, chores
Late nights, burnt out lights
Heartaches, body aches, sores
Even great memories need a sounding board
But who was I trying to kid?

I had got my answer
Nothing is impossible
When nothing is needed
When the spirit is heeded

The more you empty yourself
The more you are filled
The more you die
The more you live.
And everything that comes
Will be all you need
When all you need
Is love.

A Literary World
January 13, 2015

All the world's a stage and
I am a character in a book
Or a movie
Playing roles
But it's all make-believe
A façade
An exhibition for what it's worth.

I read all the books
In the library
And then some
And lived vicariously
Creating personas
That felt okay
Because life was not.

I got good at it
Young Doctor Kildare
The lion tamer in the circus
I was a star in first grade plays
And then the crash came.

The lights went out
For maybe two decades
Yet even then
I learned my parts
Wrote my scripts
Got by.

My reality was
Junkies, whores, radicals, flower children
And the occasional member
Of the media elite
Or at least their abandoned children
Who opened their doors and hearts
And we played together in the parks
And backyards
Eating artichokes
And escaping the horrors
Their parents had helped usher in.

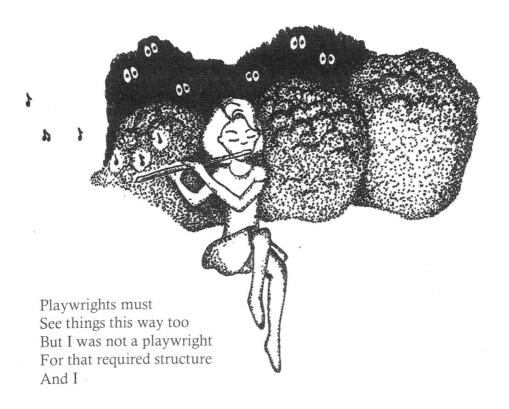

Playwrights must
See things this way too
But I was not a playwright
For that required structure
And I

Preferred free form (you see!)
Open-ended adventures
Memories
Fantasies
Floating across the Chesapeake Bay Bridge
On a hazy afternoon
The Old Laughing Lady (thanks Neil)
Late nights in Montrose
And a soft, gentle flute
That held us breathless
Awestruck
By the honesty of her notes
And the purity of her heart
(For she knew not that we were listening).

Meanwhile back at the ranch
Friends were (over)dosing themselves
Gambling with life and death
And more than once
The gamble was costly
But mostly we could
Get them moving, walk them back to life
But was any of it real?

It was the War Years
And we desperately wanted
No part of it
So we created another world
And learned too late
That our creation was for some fatally flawed.

I have learned a lot since then
Learned that fantasies are real enough
To warm cold hearts
To open blind eyes
To loosen deaf ears
But only when your fantasy
Becomes your new reality.

But isn't it wonderful
That we can use our imagination
To create scenes, story lines
That awaken long-dormant hope
That rekindle the flame
Of the promise
Of the life we all had
When we were six.

Touch
February 14, 2015

Do you see me?
Do I smell?
Can you hear me?
Do I taste well?

Four senses
All working right
But that fifth one
Causes me fright.

Seeing apparitions
Hearing voices
Tasting choices
Even mirages
Can smell so sweet.
Indeed you can stay
In your own universe
And nothing these senses offer
Has to be real.

But touch is personal
And in a world impersonal
The need for touch
Is universal.

Touch
Makes all the other senses
Come alive
And you cannot thrive
In a bubble world apart

Because you can never be sure
That seeing, hearing,
Smelling, even tasting,
Are not your fantasies,
Your imaginary friend.

Only when you are touched
Do you know
There is really someone there
Who identifies with you
As two together melding
Into one.
Are we not alone
Without the touch of love?

Don't Look Back
February 25, 2015

I looked back today
Twinged as I remembered
An old friend
Now in pain.
And uncovered a memory
Of a wild ride to Boston,
Vaguely, as did this really happen
A long, long time ago?

And the thought occurred
I have so few moments
Of such reflection
Moments I admit
That try to redefine
Our living age.

Don't look back, Zimmie said,
Or was it Pennybacker
Who sealed this message
In our hearts?
But why? We never asked.

And then it hit me.
Lot's wife looked back
And became a pillar
Of salt.
Looking back in anger
Kills our todays
And turns tomorrows
Into dark adventures.

Looking back at lost love
Denies that the love remains
To feed us every day.

The saddest words,
It might have been
Are sad
Not because of what
Was down that other road
But that you miss so much
Being offered on the road you chose.

Eyes fixed on what lies ahead
Hands and feet focused on the now.
Hearts aflutter with
The possibilities
The treasures
That we might well miss
By looking to see
Where we have been
Instead of
Where we are going ....

And we are blessed by
Our fellow sojourners
And those placed in the way
We *thought* our path was leading.

Vanity and Love
March 6, 2015

What we often call love
Is but vanity rising.
That is why when things go wrong
We get confused and say
You never loved me!
And it is true.

Vanity had met vanity
And fed on each other's imaginations.
Vanity is the illusion of love
Not the real thing.

Love is action, not hot flashes.
Love is proactive,
Focused outward.
Love is giving
That fosters real living.
How do I love thee?
Let me count the ways.
How do you love me?
I feel safe yet reenergized
For whatever tomorrow brings.

To love we have to sacrifice
Our vanities,
No longer demand
To be pleased
With our performance.

But rather we invest
Our lives, our fortunes
Our very futures
In the work of life
That love is creating
As it weaves us together.

Love builds hope
Within ourselves, beyond ourselves
Vanity not so much.

Love looks across the table
And sees herself (himself)
In the still evolving friend
Who has let go of vanity
And found new life
And together,
Transformed,
They are
Creating a team
Like oxen
Strong yet gentle
Embracing a world in need
Of the energy and power
Released through
The union of their souls.

They let love flow
In and out and around
And through the stony hearts
And the hungry hearts
Of those who want to believe
That love can touch them too.

Mirror, Mirror
April 10, 2015

Am I a mirror
Reflecting back on life
Showing Dorian Gray
The image of his vanity?

Am I a sponge
Soaking up the sweat
Of the self-absorbed?

Or am I a towel
Wiping up the messes
That careless angels
Leave behind?

Or maybe a pillow
Upon which
Golden children
Lay their heads?

Possibly I'm a podium
A sounding board
For good ideas?

I seem to have also been a ladder
Ready to be climbed
By those already at the top
Of their game.

I have been all these things
And more
I can be all things to all men
And women
They can step all over me

They hardly see me
Much less likely hear me
Surely don't recognize my existence.

One leper in ten
Looked back
To see who had pulled him
Out of death into life.

One in ten
See me for whose I am
One in ten remember
That we cannot get there
By ourselves –

One in ten know
That a partnership
Sometimes looks one-sided
Sometimes IS one-sided
Even falls apart

Because neither
Is willing
To be a doormat,
A mirror, a pillow or yes, even a towel.

True partners are willing
To fulfill each other's every need
To mold and shape success
For each other.

Best of all
Is a partnership
With two mirrors, two towels
Two hearts in awe
Of each other's joy.

Getting Our Way
April 19, 2015

It really does no good
To pout
To doubt
To chase our own dreams
Or rather our vain imaginations.

Oh, sure, you can throw a tantrum
You can find someone
Willing
To be your scapegoat
As you curse
The life
You have been given.

Well, MOST of it is more than fine
MOST of it is indeed magnetic, magical,
Even motivational
And yet
There is that one small thing
That bitter (but really sweet) pill
That dreadful vegetable
Mom always put on the plate
That you KNEW would make you
Throw up
And there it is
Larger than life
And you abhor
Your
Life

And want to escape
And just not be you for a while.

Maybe this WAS you way back when
But now you want to punish God
For letting you live
But having to love unthinkably
And so
You rebel
You tell
Yourself
It's OK
I know God will see it my way
I mean, I know my heart
I know my passions
I know my limits
I know ....

NOTHING

Other than that sick to my stomach feeling --
That same one I anticipated
From eating that dreadful vegetable --
Over a certain kind of something
Not to be named
Lest that insult to your dignity
That Jonah in the whale moment
That anticipated bitter pill
Turn out to be
Not so dreadful
After all.

Submariners
May 2, 2015

Did I really
Just drive California 1?
Did the ocean way below
Look cold and uninviting?
No boats or ships
Or even submarines
But surely plenty
Of subsurface marine life.

That's the way it is
With some people.
On the surface
They too are cold
And uninviting
Yet deep down
They really want to believe
That their stories
Matter
To somebody out there.

We tend to pass them by
To ignore their frightened
Or demoralized humanity
And so they shrink back
Into their turtle shells
And cry softly
Lest anyone hear
And know and not care.

James Robertson
Is such a man.
Son of the beloved

Veterinarian
Who plied his trade
With the racing community.

James worked
With tile and marble
Until his legs gave out.

Now he sits in his chair on wheels
Keeps calm with two pints a day
And waits --
For SSI?
For the county caregivers?
Not a chance!

He is moving on soon
To make a new start
And his eyes lit up
To know a stranger
Just stopping for water
And a stretch
Wanted to know his story.

His eyes were kind
And he made my day
By being truly human
And showing me
The unstoppable hope
In his beating heart
That somewhere, soon,
His life will turn around
His good works continue
And his soul find comfort.

Writing History One Day at a Time
May 4, 2015

On the way to tomorrow
Today happened,
And today
Was a roller coaster --
Which is to say
We rolled out of bed
Grabbed a bite
With our new friends
In Big Sur
Then stopped at a bridge
And marveled
At the power of the sea.

A pause to refresh our souls
We chose Point Lobos
Where there are no wolves
But there are otters and sea lions
Or maybe harbor seals
And sea birds galore!

Then the trek to Gibson Beach
Where Abba Modern
Was shooting a music video
To dance before the King
And celebrate the Kingdom of Light

And so we did celebrate
With yoga (sorta)
And cartwheels.

Imagine the seals
Clapping
As we laughed and loved
The sea water spraying our legs
As we ran to the stairway.

It was a big deal
So our hearts could heal
And our souls refresh.

What a day!
The air was clean
The water surprisingly warm
As we engaged the charm
Of Pacifica!

Level

May 10, 2015

As we remember
Who we really are
Deep down
Where we came from
Who molded and shaped us
Into their own image
Before we realized
Those were our baby teeth
And we had to grow our own
Balls

We know
Instinctively
Our mates
Those who came
From where we evolved
Even those
Who speak our hidden language

We want to say No!
We are not of that root
We evolved, died
Only to live anew
In the world
We created for ourselves
But we know
That's not true
Entirely

And so
When we find
A living soul
With our own history,
Our own destiny
Becomes clouded
With memories
Of who we thought
We only ONCE were.

We are back to square one
In a trapezoidal world
Seeking a level
That fulfills our dreams
On a foundation
That just feels right.

Note: Written while dancing at the legendary Elbo Room in San Francisco.

Pain
May 11, 2015

I met a guy the other day
Had a shiny vintage white
Convertible
With real chrome bumpers
And hand pedals
So he could drive
Without using legs
That no longer work.

He looked happy
Said it just took a bit
To remember which hand
Controls the accelerator
And which controls the brakes.

What if, I mused,
I am soon faced
With that choice?
Ride on without dancing legs
Or curl up
And die?

The answer should be obvious
Life is likely much more
Stimulating
Than the alternative
And is it ego
Or heartbreak
That would make such a choice
Less than automatic?

There is nothing worse
Than living alone
And in reality
We all die alone
But of course
A living death
Is worse than both.

But then there is that dying life
Out of a single glorious moment
My friend Russ lives such a life

Flailing about it seems at times
And yet announcing to the world
He has been STANDING

And what a guy
Created a magazine (later a zine)
From scratch
He interviews the stars
The up and comers
The living
As he is so alive

And no one
Demonstrated the dying life
Better than my beloved
Who when confronted with the worst
Merely said, "Oh, darn!"

But am I willing
Should the need arise
To give up that ultimate ego trip
To give up the wheel
Or at least give up the wheels
And trade them in for steel ones?

Maybe
I will be spared such a choice
I am no hero
I have no aspirations
To be oohed and cooed and wooed
As if I were a plant
Or a piece of antique furniture

Or worse, ignored
Left alone
For why would anyone even care?
Or dare
Endure
My search for a cure
Or at least an alternative
To immobility?

I don't see the benefit
I don't feel the hope
That extending by artifice
Would enable joy to flow
From such a wounded warrior.
But who am I to judge?
Is it my right?

There is really no point in such
Ponderings
No reason to look beyond
The joys of today

And yet ....

Going Home
July 6, 2015

Someone once said
You can't go home again
But I say
Home is a state of mind
That sometimes
Happens
In familiar haunts.

Life is a journey
That should include campfires
As it is sometimes around campfires
We find the comforts
That remind us of home.
We went home the other night.
Back to fireflies and fireworks
And home cooking
And stories about family and "friends"
Whom we rarely (never) see.
Time stopped, stood still
Or maybe we had traveled back
To a gentler, simpler era
When everything was supposed to be
Better.

And that night it was
Though we have hazy memories
That our first trip through
Had been a bumpier ride.

How we (and they) have grown!
How old wounds have healed.
How older arguments
Have no power to do harm
Today.

But home cannot be a residence
For our work is calling us
Back to the frontier
And yet

Home is in our veins
And what remains
Instills within us
The energy
To patiently walk through
Our new landmines
With eyes that sense every danger
And new-found wisdom
That peace can emerge
In our hearts

So we will know
What steps to take
And what steps to avoid.

Dual/Duel Unrealities
August 23, 2015

Let's say
You had a plan
And a backup plan
But with two plans
There are always two
Who are looking for a plan
And when the two plans collide
Sparks fly.

You lit the match
By having a backup plan
Others poured gasoline on the fire
They did not light
But did not put out either.

And now, like the Olympic flame
No one can put it out
It festers, waiting for new fuel
Embers hot as hell
Containing all the venom
Of a nest of water moccasins.

Adaptation
Modification
Blues
News
Not forthcoming

But how does the cookie crumble?
How does one divide the baby
Without bloodshed?

Like a movie with two scripts
You haven't got a Clue
So whaddya do
When the rain turns to thunder
And lightning chases you down the block?

You MIGHT say
At least this is not a tornado
And then the whirlwind picks you up
And throws you against the fence
And you
Shake the dust off your feet
And your shirt and pants
And you dance.

For as Snoopy said
To live is to dance
And there is a chance
The others will join in
And begin
Anew.

Infinite Galaxies
August 29, 2015

We used to think
How far is a star
How wonderful you are
And all that shooting star rot.

We used to think people we loved
Were stars
Until
We worked with them
Played with them
Danced with them
Laughed with them
Cried with them
Almost died with them
Took a long ride with them
Allied with them
In the big battle for our own souls.

As we grow we begin to know
These friends are not mere stars
But infinite galaxies.

Truth is at first
We maybe thought, ho hum,
Another ex-bum come
To take up space
And waste my time

Or maybe not!

For we ought
To be accustomed
To the infinite
Who is all around us
And in us.
We ought to know
That our encounters
Are opportunities
To expand our horizons
To grow in love and awe.

Made in the divine image
Means
Not simple
Not to put in a box
Not to cast aside
Like broken toys.

Rather let us converse
On a hillside
Let us look at the clouds
While lying in the green grass
Let us feel the Infinite
That connects us.
Let us be free to be
Living, giving trees
Of life.

Infinite partials
A friend once said
Coming together only in community
As we build a unity
Out of diverse perverse
Maybe even cursed
Erased yesterdays.

To Hell and Maybe Back
August 31, 2015

Hell is
Not knowing
If your loved one is all right
Not knowing if she took flight
And crashed and burned
Or if she just learned
Some news too hard to bear.

But because you care
How dare
The universe
Not keep you posted
Not let you be the
Knight in rusted armor.

Here I am to save the day
Mighty Mouse in the house
But what is there to do
But wait
And hope
And wonder
Why
You
Were kept in the dark
When all you wanted
Was to light her way
Through the dark forest
Slay her dragons
Build her a home
Water her garden

Serenade her in the misty morning
Take away all her pain --

And yet what does she gain
If you do all the work?

Then it hits you
That lonesome valley
Full of shadows
Is her path to freedom

And all you can do
Is keep watch
And cheer her on
And hope
She remembers your name
When she beats the maze
Emerges from the fire
Cleansed and ready
To live and love and grow.

And you know
That love
Does not seek its own
Is not puffed up
May go unrewarded
May find itself
Applauding from afar.

But on the other hand
Once in a while
Once, twice maybe in a lifetime
The life you save may be your own.

Though you know you really
Just stood in the gap
Holding your breath

Hoping

She had enough love
To win her war
And will track you down
Hold your hand
Kiss your face

Trace

The lines in your forehead
That widened and deepened
While she was fighting for her life
And, seeing the joy in your heart
That her victory brings,
Will say, Tag, You're IT
And lead you on a merry chase
Through the fertile fields
Of tomorrow.

What If?
September 21, 2015

What if
Everything you had told yourself
About yourself
Was turned upside down?

What if
Instead of being a catalyst
You were just a parasite
Nobody needed your help
To fulfill their dreams
And the dreams you did help fulfill
Turned into nightmares?

What if
Your path was to be very different?
What if
You looked into the mirror
And saw an ugly soul
Angry at the world
And unwilling to change for the better?
What should you do with that information?

Who would you dare ask
If you were wise or crazy
Or just lazy
In the face of trouble
That you brought upon yourself?

What if you realized
You were in the way?
Would you be brave
And walk away?

Or would you find new ways
To fake a good reputation
To try to keep the truth from coming out
That you are a fraud
A charlatan
A mischief maker
A creep?

What if
After going through all of the excuses
All of the ruses you imagined
You then realized
You were deceiving yourself
Out of fear
That all of this was true?

Are you really ready to quit
Based on a new backstory
You invented
Because the times got tough
And doubt was trying to creep in
And spoil the joy
And kill the dreams
And hurt those around you
More than you would ever know?

So what!
Maybe you are all those things
Maybe there is not a decent bone in your body

Maybe everything you touch
In the end
Falls apart?

But what if it doesn't?
What if by hanging on
Getting back on track
Keeping the faith
You find
In a few days
Miracles you never expected
Solutions to problems beyond your grasp
New energy
New vision
New love.

Why quit when you are behind?
The race is still on
And there is much to be done
And all you have to do
Is get up, keep moving, and love.

If what you believe
If who you are
If how you live
Is valid
The results will show
When you reach the finish line
And blast off into a new dimension --
And you never saw THAT coming either!

Setting Sail
October 7, 2015

You'd think this house was an airport
People are flying in and out
All the time
Turning on a dime
Or maybe a quarter of a year
Or so.

Maybe it's a bus terminal
At least during South by Southwest
When the very, very best
Of all the travelers
Find their way here
And never really go home again
For they have learned
That going forward
Means
Even the old has become new
And the next destination
Even if to places familiar in a way
Is unexplored.

What we know
Is
That lives change for the better
While living in a sanctuary
A place where people believe
Dreams really can come true
And act accordingly.

What we hope
Is
That our own future will be as bright
As that of those who have come and gone
And those who are soon going
Knowing
Their lives will never be the same
And that the flame
Now burning in their souls
Is purging that which is unprofitable
And soldering the new superstructure into place.

It is from this launch pad
Or maybe it really is a marina
That we too hope to set sail
Someday soon
Maybe next June (or sooner)
If time permits
For we too have dreams
We too seek adventures
And a whole new world.

Ready for Prime Time
December 1, 2015

The little things that no one notices
The harbingers of positive change
The troubadours of tomorrow's truth
They come gently
Sing softly
So that only YOU will hear
The messages they announce for your life.

The times you went to bed hungry
Not for physical food.
The nights you slept in tears
The sheets burning your soul
As you wandered in your dreams
To places like palaces and palisades
In search of …

The return to the daily grind
Almost seems inevitable
And yet
You know you are already ground into hamburger
Fried on a beach somewhere exotic
Spiced with authentic seasonings
And ready to be served
As you serve by sharing
The poems of your heart and soul.

So why languish on the Group W bench?
Why grow stale through pointless labors?

Why not soar?
You earned the right
You fought the fight
Your heart is bursting
And your visions will delight
No need for fright
You are already in the spotlight
And the song's beginning
It's your cue

And you
Want more time (Am I ready?)
Want more space (Are they really out there?)
Want a better band (But they will show up!)
Want more security (When your security is within!)
Want affirmations that you are not crazy
For following your dream.

And yet all you need
Is already inside
The affirmation of the heart
The applause of the soul
The knowledge
That your true security comes
From getting OUT THERE
And living the life you chose.

Top: Songwriter *Josh Halverson*.
Bottom: *Duggan* with *Rainn Rice*.

Top: *Adrienne Essmann* and *Amanda "Awethu" Blain*. Adrienne is back in college seeking a business degree. Amanda is teaching yoga and blogging "Empower through Vulnerability."

Bottom: *Ryan Koronich* is playing guitar in Austin.

Music on the Dugout Stage between the live oaks, SXSW 2018.

Top: *The Holy Child*, the longtime Dugout "house band."

Bottom: *La Fonda* from Seattle was a last-minute addition to our outstanding lineup.

Music in the Dugout living room: Jackie Venson's birthday party.

Top: *Jackie Venson* leads the jam.

Bottom: The legendary *D Madness* on lead guitar (photo by
Dugout denizen *Rainn Rice*).

Top: *Jen Chilkotowsky*, community builder; *Dion Evans*, music producer. **Bottom:** *Robert Alarcon*, lead singer, The Holy Child; *Allyssa Milan*, poet, performance artist, and muse.

Dancing at the Dugout. Top: *Chef Scott* and *Jen Chilkotowsky*; *Fernando Rafa Sanchez* from The Holy Child. **Bottom:** *Duggan* dancing with daughter *Melody*; *Judson McKinney* serenades.

Heart of Danger
January 3, 2016

As February approaches
Fear not Cupid's arrow
But rather the slings and arrows
Of strangers and friends
Who treat your heart
As target practice
Or a punching bag.

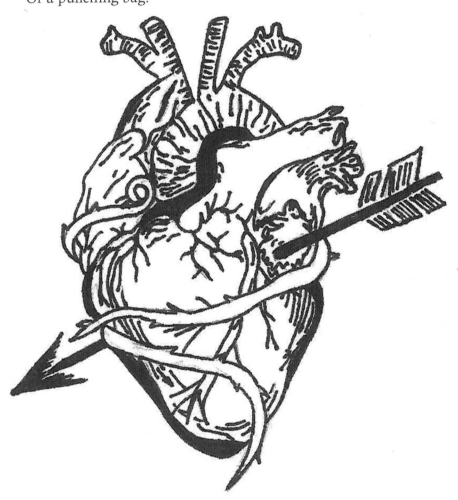

The healthy heart is a field
Where love grows
Absorbing hurt, hate, and hypocrisy
And turning doubt into trust.

The damaged heart, though
Lacks the clear, consistent beat
That defines the universe around us
And sorts through the noise
To nurture everyone
Within its reach.

The prophet exhorts us
To guard our hearts
Which reminds us
We are under attack
At least now and then.

And when
We open ourselves up
To love
We must not give
The combination that unlocks
This treasured vessel
To anyone who will not cherish
And nurture the soul
That our heart guards.

For the heart is a dangerous thing
To fall into the wrong hands.

Familiar Faces
January 10, 2016

Hail, fellow, well met
There's a face I won't forget
And a name comes to mind
(Often with prompting)
Always just in time.

The ritual
The trite sayings
Betray the lie
There is no you and I
No history, no mystery
No adventures to recall
Truth is I hardly know you at all.

Have we lost the art
Of conversations over tea
Even as we sit together
To quaff a brew
And watch "Friends" or "the game"?

Can we put down our cell-phone computers long enough
To hear how little Johnny Junior hit a home run
Or that neighbor Bill has become a master carpenter?

Everyone has gifts or something to share
But we
Dare

Not
Listen

Everyone can learn from the stories of our lives
But we
Dare not
Tell them.

Pretty soon
We no longer know them.

Over time, familiar faces fade
But the stories, the songs
The heartbreaks, the celebrations we share
Will remain
(Believe in love).

Four Seasons in a Week
March 19, 2016

Austin South by South West
Four seasons in a week
Hot heat to rain clouds
To a cold wind
Blowing the visitors
Back home.

The closing of an Era
The end of the line
The beginning
Of something
As yet undefined.

See ya next year
Isn't gonna happen
Because time requires
And life desires
To take
The vision
On the road.

Just how, even where
Remains off the drawing board
But one suspects
The seeds
Are already sown
And the unknown
Gardens
Are waiting to be watered

As the Gardener
Is now at work
Breaking up the soil.
The troops are ready
For the prince of peace
Or at least his envoy
Bringing joy --
Or really just a mirror
To the joy that lies
Within the hearts
Of this tribe of lovers
So easily disheartened
Distracted
By the petty politics
Of division.

So, we subtract the stress
And add the blessings
And multiply the numbers
Of those who cast
Their lives aside
In order to receive
Dancing orders
Or rather opportunities
To teach others
The way of the dance.

Instant Karma
March 20, 2016

Be instant
In season and out
Of season.
Not my words
But words of wisdom
That constrain self-absorption
And challenge us
To awareness and empathy

To be present
To give out of our need
To walk and chew gum
At the same time.

So many cry for affirmation
So few even notice
The soul behind the face
The opportunity for grace
To reach inside
Expose what they hide
Dry the tears that they cried
Without invading their space.

We tend
To focus on ourselves
We are so scattered
Keeping our own center
Is such a hurdle

And yet
We forget
The human signposts
Who would show us the way
If we only paid
Attention.

Our lives
Are not our own
We breathe
We drink
We share space
We are not alone.

We thrive
On cross pollination
On the exchange of hope
And the recognition
Of our own humanity
Our own divinity
Our own joy
In the faces
We all too often
Ignore.

Convergence
April 8, 2016

Springing along
Racing the clock
June is wedding month
Time for new beginnings
New treasures
To be uncovered
New fields
To be explored.

Will I get there on time?
Can't be late for the ceremony
And yet
What steps to take?

Is this the end
A farewell to arms
And legs
Or a vision
Of a promised hand
And a new partnership
A new mothership?

Or will the old one do
As a launching pad
A proving ground
Where the final tests
Prepare us for tomorrows
Beyond our wildest dreams?

The planets may align
But that's not the sign.
Implanted in our mind
Is the grand design
For the day ahead
And nothing more.

Perhaps faint visions
Of a future that may yet be
Yet that fateful step
We have to take
As did Kal-El
And the other super heroes.

Leaving the building just in time
Requires a leap of faith
Because unlike them
We don't know
When the old building will implode.

We also know not
Where we are going
And yet
Go we must
Or gather dust
And rust.

Trust
Is that confidence
That we heard the word

Got the memo
Knew change was coming
If we wanted to keep living
By dying to our old flesh and bone

Volunteering for the journey
Because we know
We are not alone

Good gifts will follow
As we follow in the way
Our feet are taking us.

Proactive
May 16, 2016

Too much of our lives
We are reactive.
We respond to those
Who seek to shape our paths
Guide our steps,
Fit us into their mold.

It starts with our first cry
And we are socialized
Into families whose members
Stake their claims on our hearts
And strongly desire
That we learn, thus affirm, their ways.

As we grow, though,
We find other patterns,
Other adventures,
Other people
With whom we intertwine.

We grow to become
A reflection
Of what we have found
To be good, or submissive
Or even overbearing
As we are really sharing
A common acceptance
Of safety and comfort and grace
Or for some a sad assumption
Of being forever lost in space.

But once in a while
We step outside our reflexes
Recheck our secret indexes
And pause from our role playing
To seek out our own core
And build up our own store,
Our brand, our very special identity.

Are we disappointed
In how hard it is
To extricate ourselves
From the daily routine
The social scene
To have a date
With ourselves?

For revelation comes in solitude
Birthed in our lonesome valleys
And hidden hills
The thrills!
Or the chills
If we fail to celebrate
Fail to create
In those quiet mornings
Or silent sunsets
As we go.

Do we even like
The person we see
When we are learning to be
The future our true self
Might bring about?

Can we shout
Our rooftop blessing
Confessing
That only we can give
The love we discover
Deep within
The crevices of our hearts?

Hearts we all too often fail to water
Fail to listen to every beat
Fail to follow where they lead
Fail to celebrate our freedom.

Then we suddenly remember
That our slowly dying ember
Just needs a little fire
A purposeful desire
To aspire
To light the night.

Second Chances

July 16, 2016

Not everyone
Gets to see
How his life might
Have turned out
Not everyone
Gets a second chance
At growing up.

Yet too many
Are stuck
In a plastic, make-believe world
In which adulthood is
Measured by wealth accumulation
Or parenthood, or fame.

Emotions paralyze our souls
When violence interferes
With our peace.

We stop growing
Stop being childlike
Stop dreaming
Die inside.

But life
Is for living
And forgiving

And when we cast off
The pain guilt and shame

Those secret walls of our secret prison
Fall away

And we are as one
Frozen in time

Newly thawed out

Free to become

Ourselves.

Celebrate
September 25, 2016

It's six am
The party's sorta over
But you feel
The cool breeze
And the breaking sunshine.

Time for a walk
Time to chill
Time to absorb
The magnitude
Of sharing our divinity
From here to infinity
As the magick elixir
That is Zoe (life)
Of, by, and for you
Explodes the myth
That you are too old to fly

And time goes by
Slowly
As you savor
The flavor
Of the morning dew,
And the quiet,
Broken by a bird song
Celebrating the rain
That is soon to fall.

And so we dance
Catching raindrops on our tongues
Forever young

Bananas, raisins, and chia seeds
Await our return to the table

And we are able
Once sated with fruit and (well) tacos
To settle in for a morning nap

And arise to celebrate
Our next adventure

In the ongoing joy
That is the gift of life.

Gardening
March 11, 2017

We are supposed to be
Children
All our lives
Even as we handle grownup
Things
But hurt and lies and vanity
Make us doubt
Our childlike nature
And so we pursue
Things that make us
Jaded.

Faded
Are our memories
Of when we were
Free
To be
To explore and see
The beauty
Created all around us
And in each other
And in ourselves.

Most times
We wear a grownup face
Which is to say
We adopt conventions
Full of intentions
To live and let give
But not to give
Ourselves away.

All the while
We starve
Our childlike heart
Behind the art
Of hiding
Our vulnerability
And our reality
Gets submerged
In the mishmash
Of "getting along."

We can't be strong
Because our power
Our joy
Is an offense or a threat
Or just an ugly reminder
Of the lives not dared
In the faces
Of those around us.

Some challenge, some boast
But the most
Good
We can do
Is to disarm
Those hurting the most
To be so real
They dare to enter
Where only fools survive
That is, to come fully alive.

Joni was wrong
In her song
We can't get ourselves
Home
By striving, conniving
Scheming, or even dreaming.
We just have to let go
So we can grow
Younger again.

The Garden never left us
We ran away
But today
I say
Click your heels
Stop making deals
Stop spinning wheels
And FEEL

Touch, smell, listen, and sing
Get into the swing
And dance
And the romance
Of breathing deep
Will show the yellow path
Back.

The Unknown Soldier
March 27, 2017

I soldier on
Alone
Or so I sometimes lie
For I
Have
A companion
Who guides my steps
Tries
To bridle my tongue
To measure my words
And often I follow
That wisdom.

So when we
Open ourselves to strangers
The dangers
Lie
When we act
Out of our emotions
Rather than wait
For the peace
That shows
The secret door
That reveals the benefits
We did not know
We were about to find.

Last night
Surprises followed
From obeying the choice

To build a brotherhood
And so much
That transpired
Was the result
Of yielding to the plan.

Seek always
The highest call
But not by your own vanities
For our biases
Cloud our vision.

Listen to the gentle wind
And open your eyes
To the opportunities
To give and receive
And marvel
At the energy
At the revelation
At the wisdom
Unmasked
And shared.

Some may say
Coincidence
Yet you know
Something -- or someone -- else
Was conducting the orchestra.

Three Hundred Sixty-Five Suns
May 21, 2017

Some people measure time
In years
Birthdays, anniversaries, seasons
But each year has three hundred
And sixty-five suns (some a bonus day)
And each day presents a brand-new adventure.

People wonder
How do we live together
Years, decades, three score and more?
What is the secret?
A young man answered
"Quality, not quantity,"
And therein hangs the tale.

Each day is its own crown jewel
For us to display brightly
In all of our travels
Inward and otherwise.
Each day may bring something new
Someone new,
A new you?

Why do we measure time in years – or at all?
Time is instant – always moving forward
As should we.
And yet
So many say Blue Monday
Or Friday I'm in Love
Or Tuesdays and Saturdays
Or Eight Days a Week –

Now there's a guy who gets it!

Not excited about each new day?
Then check your life
Or check your attitude.

Live with gratitude
Drink deeply as from an oasis well.

Know that each soul you meet
Was crafted by a master designer
And has secret joys hiding sometimes
In the nooks and crannies
Of their being
That not even they had known before
Existed
Until you provided the key
That unlocked their hearts.

If, that is, you took the time given you
To do the job.

Uprooted
August 25, 2017

I came "home"
To a mostly empty house
Packing has begun
And I have no place yet to go.
But I know
Something will turn up
That makes sense.
At least I hope so.

There is something horrid
About being uprooted
My daughters felt it
When we had to move
And move again …

Lost memories, lost friends
Lost opportunities
Sometimes cloud the gains
That await the open-hearted
And yet the road is dark
Until the star comes
To light the way.

Today
I ponder
Did I do something wrong?
Did some evil force want me gone?
Or am I being liberated
To travel to new heights
Begin a new mission
Or just fade away?

One day for sure
There will be no more tomorrows
At least on this plane
But then again
What if this trip
Is just the prelude?

One thing I know for sure
The adventure of life
Is to be lived wide open
Learning as we go
I know
I have learned much
And spoken too much
And listened not enough
Some of the time.

As I contemplate the path
Or paths that lie ahead
I do not dread
Even being dead
Unless I am still breathing.

Questions and Gifts

August 31, 2017

There are questions
We dare not ask
Dare not answer
Dare not even dream.

There are answers
We did not want to hear
Do not know how to handle
Cannot be.

Down the road we chose
We find ourselves in the throes
Of confusion, doubt, and fear
Until we remember
This is OUR road
And it leads to somewhere
We ought to be.

Life is but one long battle
To get above the struggle
And focus on the now
Yet only when we ignore the struggle
Will we receive what we need.

Those questions, those answers
Were not for us anyhow.
Distractions
That ought not bog us down.

There is no struggle
Once we remember
All our provisions are at hand.

Sparrows marvel
Lilies sing
As they glory
In the gifts WE receive

Gifts that for all too long
We failed to see

Let alone believe
They were ours.

The Promise of the Reel

December 9, 2017

Dancing

Is one of our oldest sports
Never celebrated as such
Yet much loved
By doers and watchers alike.

We dance to celebrate life.
Zorba!

We dance to seduce and subdue
But better is the mating dance
When two recognize their partnership
Soaring over clouds
Through the driving rain
On mountaintops
And in life's darkest valleys.

We dance to music played loud
We dance to the quiet of
A hidden field
The secret garden
The wide open spaces

We dance on our beds
We dance in our heads
We dance and prance
And sometimes our dance
Goes into hiding
When we are afraid

But the dance of life
Is stronger than all our fears.

No matter how many years
We cried buckets of tears
When we dance
Our hearts glow
And we know
We will dance on our own graves!

On the Precipice
January 17, 2018

I saw an airplane
Falling off a cliff
But rescued by thick mud
That held its wheels in place
So the people aboard
Could scurry off
Carefully
To safe havens.
Close call!

Today one dear to me
Reported that she was
Still alive.
Boulder on the highway
Just before the dawn
Last minute swerve
Clipped a tire,
Bounced off the guardrail
Overlooking a deep crevasse
Bounced across two lanes
To the safety of a ditch
And then a semi
Hit the rock, sent it flying
To a spot she had been standing
Just before a passing trucker
Whisked her tear-filled eyes
Into safety.

How many times have we
Been in grave danger
Unexpectedly

Through no fault of our own
About to face extinction
When all of a sudden
We are on dry land
As if transported by magic
Or angels (messengers)
Of what we all too often
Dare to deem coincidence.

Sometimes an open door
Just looks like
Part of the landscape
And we do not see
It is really a portal
Another doorway
To the land of
Joy.

Oh, boy!
You never imagined
This.
You never thought yourself
Worthy
Or blessed or even
Humble enough
To surrender your fears
To the one who loves
You.

It is not good to be alone
No one is an island
And yet
When the ferry comes
Will we be on board?

Again today I heard
From a little bird
That a stubborn heart
Got locked up
Again
Just a little more time
A little more cleansing
Another chance
To live in grace.

Where is YOUR place?
Dare you go there?
Is your institution one
Where the doors are not locked?
I mean, why lock the doors
When the inmates fear their freedom
More than their bondage?

And there it is –
You stand on the precipice
You look down
Or up.

You have a parachute
Or a hot air balloon
You can go
You know
And your destination,
Your destiny,
Is that pot of gold
At the end of your heart
That joy you never thought
You were entitled to
But one day realized
That miracles happen
When we let them.

The Urgency of Rest
March 20, 2018

So you finished the last race
You stayed the course
You got through the hard stuff
You knew it was time to rest.

But you know that tomorrow
Is really three or five
Days away.
And while there is much to do
The urgency
Of doing something new
Something unknown
Does not require
That you jump through hoops
Or get ahead of time.

Sufficient to each day
Is the opportunity you have
To breathe,
To accept the day that is
And to trust
That the day that must be
Shall come.

So the only true urgency
Is the urgency of rest.

Each day every way
Is prepared for you to
Respond
To the universe
Out of that rest.

A wise woman once said
Never let the urgent
Interfere with the important.
And yet what is more important
Than being ready to act
When opportunity knocks?

Thus, the urgency of rest
Is the test
The preparation
For whatever tomorrow brings
The things
To do that are true
To you.

Separation
March 26, 2018

My mother never knew her mother.
My grandfather never knew his father.
My own life began when I was nearly four.
I remember nothing prior to learning to read.
Nothing.

My stepdaughter was born
While her sister was dying
And so was sent away for a time
To be raised by strangers.

My mother was sent to her preacher grandpa
And became a missionary.

My grandpa's mom died
When he was eight
And he was sent to boarding school
Became a fiddle-playing barber
And father of nine.

My stepdaughter had a rough road
And today is winning the little battles
That alienation had once taken from her.

And as for me?
I got lucky --
Had both
Yet neither.
But this is just the prelude.
The story is not about me.

We are talking thousands,
Millions, as it were
Of broken homes, lost lives,
Hurting children
And desperate parents
Crying out for trusted love.

Cannon fodder, political footballs
Soon to be replaced with robots.
The dead men who rule over us
Soon will no longer need their labor.

The best and brightest
As with horses and oxen
May be kept around as souvenirs
While the others
When their strength is no longer needed
Will be left to fend for themselves.
Or, worse, set against each other
For the amusement of the demigods
And their entourages.

Unless..

Unless we stop hating each other
Use our TWO ears (and two eyes)
More than our one tongue ...

For the tongue, it is said, is a fire
A world of evil that corrupts the whole body
Full of poison and often forked
Speaking praises and curses together.

Unless we become peacemakers ...

Unless we esteem even those we have
Condemned
Without even walking a furlong
In their blue suede shoes.

Unless we first love the unlovely
The ones we used to call names
And snicker about

Unless we listen, and look, and learn
And having cleansed our own hearts
See how we might cleanse theirs.

Living Free in the Face of Extinction
April 27, 2018

In the police state that exists
Ambulances too are the enemy
You see them rolling up the driveway
Hauling away the corpses
Making room for new future pilgrims...

You are old, washed up
No longer of benefit
Cost-ineffective
Worthless
To those who lack divinity
Or, to be truthful, humanity.

They don't factor in
The value of story
Or the wisdom of time
Or the power of love.
They are automatons
Bookkeepers turned bosses
Bean counters
Who operate as if under orders
To cut costs, make room
For tomorrow's supplicants
Because THEIR JOB
As they define it
Is to share the poverty of spirit
That has led us to war
Against our own flesh, blood
Bone and spirit.

So our job
While we still have breath
Is to rally the living
To bang loud cymbals
To keep the drumbeat going
To liberate souls
From obeisance to the death marchers
Who see humanity
As interlopers
Abusers
Planet killers
By their very existence.

But they have deemed themselves
Protectors
With the power to silence
Even snuff out
Carbon units who do not bow the knee
To their self-assumed authority
That also entitles them
As planet saviors
As economists
To special extra shares
Of their own myopic shrinking pie.

Meanwhile, hidden from their view
The Tree of Life is feeding
A brand-new revolution
A revival of the soul
A band of brothers, sisters
And, yes, others in between
Who celebrate truths
Among fellow travelers
On a secret path
Laid out with painstaking detail
That transform our weaknesses

Into the glue that builds an army
Of singers and dancers
Who celebrate
The rhythm of the universe
And melt away the blinders
That have kept souls bound
Cogs in a Malthusian death machine
Allies with their own abusers.

But that day is soon over
For love always triumphs
Simply by the power of joy
Which is stronger even
Than the power of death
And all of death's Zombie soldiers.

So we live not in fear
Of the bean counters
The self-righteous, self-appointed
Prudes
And libertines
Both of whom see the living
As threats to their own god
The love of darkness.

They deny our common bond
As inheritors of
The divine nature
By which we all were stamped
That makes each snowflake
Each human
Unlike any other
And capable of creation
Or destruction.

So which way are YOU wired?

Check your energy,
Check your heart.

Celebrate each day
As a special gift
Each member of your tribe
Who energizes your own
Humanity, divinity, joy.

And celebrate especially
Those who at the end of life
Are so full of life
Their joy overflows into you
And bathes you in the river
That no bean counter
Can ever appropriate
Can ever control its flow.

Cooperation through communication
Not coercion
Is the key to the harmonics of life
That will change our futures
From fear to freedom.

The awakening is upon us
The mandala of giving
Out of our need
And thereby receiving
Those things that enable us
To live free yet strongly connected
To the energy of life
That reveals the wonders
Even in those
Others
Had deemed
Deplorable
Or alien
Or *passé*.

Do unto others
May take time to work
But time is the illusion
That death is nearer.

And life is timeless
We have always been
(Ali figured that one out)

And our infinity
Is our divinity
Combined with our humanity.

How shall we then live?

The Beginning Is Now
June 9, 2018

The war is over.
We won.
The house that could not
Be home
Became a home
For the homeless
And the homesick.

The family shattered by death
Had to find new life
On their on
And with considerable help
From a few who knew
The bombs had taken
Those they loved the most.

Sure, we won, but the cost
The hurt, the anger, the pain
Remain
And Humpty
May have been
One bad egg.

It was not the king's horses
Nor the king's men
Who oversaw the reconstruction
That may have really been
The last great gift.

The old carcass
Suddenly
Became alive
And the body who had labored

And the soul set free
Joined
Became a new being
To be shaped and molded
By the not-at-all-random souls
Who joined the fray
Even if for but a moment.

The magic was real
The ghosts were holy
The challenges mammoth at times

The music shaped us
Helped us see
How to be
Ourselves
And to recognize
Our shared opportunity
To reach beyond our fears
And see tomorrows.

And now that tomorrow has come
The end is over.
The beginning
Is now.

But where to begin?
And what to do?
Transmute into furniture
To be used and thrown away
Or cast into the fire?
Didn't think so!

Sure, a moment of rest,
A few days in paradise.
Recuperation, planning

To set sail
On that final journey
That never ends?
Or find a final home
And rot away slowly
Armed only with fading
Memories?

Not either.

The little engine that could
May one day run out of fuel

But the Son Taxi
Or sunny D
Is still for hire

Or, rather, assignment
And looking already ahead
To the next adventure.

Diamonds and Iron

July 18, 2018

They played the All-Star game yesterday
Everyone came out to play
On the diamond.

Diamonds are forever, said James Bond
But forever in this life can be abruptly altered.
Shocks us to see how much we faltered
To be real together
When time stood still.

That lump of coal named Billy Joe
Still looks forward to becoming a diamond
Knowing he has been pretty darn rough

And we all know our inner Billy Joe
And fail to see
That we really are clean and clear
We just have to turn on the switch.

But you do know
That diamonds are but our crude attempts
To honor the glory of the stars
For the promise has long been
That we and they are one for one.

But on the other hand
We are also as the grains of sand
The chaff that falls to land
Turned as to stone from fear
That our gifts might not be well received.

The choice is there for all
The stars or the sand
But we who are smug
Who neither sharpen others
Nor let their rough edges polish ours
Will never become the stars
Not even the diamonds
We were created to become.

But here's a clue
Love is the motor oil
Without which
Diamond polishing
Aka coal squeezing
Is painful mostly to our egos.
Love is also that which cleaves
Without the pain of being cut.
Get out of that rut
And let love do its work
And really, truly shine forever.

Preparing To Die

October 11, 2018

They say elephants
Knowing they are dying
Leave their herd behind
And wander away
Alone.

So too in tribes
When a member
Had lost her usefulness
She sacrificed her old age
So that the tribe
Was spared a burden.

Solitary confinement
Even in a prison
Of your own making
Forces you
To deal with the depths
Of your darkness

And for some, the already dead,
This prison is a relief as
They no longer have to deal
With the ugliness around them.

At least they are alone
Except for their familiar
Demons.

Yet sometimes they hear
Another voice.

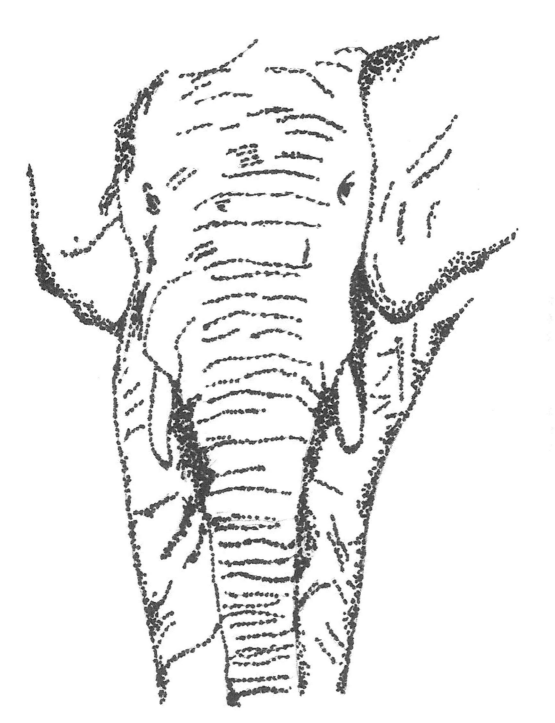

Acknowledgments

So many have helped make this book possible. It would take an entire book to thank them all. Of course, I am thankful for everyone mentioned in this book, and for so many others whose names are not listed here. Just too many stories to tell – until the next book.

I want to thank my longtime friend (and former SonShine Inn employee) Kathie Scriven, who furiously edited the prose sections of the book and insisted I write a Preface, shorten my overlong sentences (poets do that), and improve the story's flow.

I also must thank my former boss and longtime friend Mark St. John Couhig, who helped me navigate the publishing universe to get comparison prices, determine the book format, and so much more.

I cannot yet comprehend the total contribution of publicist and friend Elise Krentzel, who kicked my butt and told me I needed to get serious about marketing, her own forte. I am only hopeful at this juncture that I will be able to utilize more of her great skills in getting this book out to a broader audience.

Finally, without the kindness and consistency of Hilary Kuhlmey as a collaborator in book design and production – in addition to her drawings that grace many of these pages – this book would not exist.

And, yeah, gotta thank my Source. Peace, joy, love, and understanding all stem from the Infinite, the Designer of the Infinite Galaxies I have loved.

Artist Hilary Kuhlmey

I was the student who was always scribbling pictures in my notebook while the teacher was talking. I was the scholar who would write song lyrics instead of studying in the library. I was the schoolgirl who listened to music to bear through homework, so distracted by singing along that I completely lost sight of the work I was doing. I've always been an artist. When I didn't even know it myself, all the signs were there.

In 2013, I started full-heartedly pursing a singing career and casually displayed my paintings in art shows. My singing seemed to be taking off effortlessly, so I followed the momentum and built my life around making a living as a singer and singing coach.

In 2018, I experienced devastating health issues that limited my ability to sing. I had spent the past four years building a career around singing, and now here I was struggling to use my voice. After months of trying to push through my pain, I finally surrendered to what was happening.

The summer of 2018, I took a step back from my music career and allowed my body to truly rest and heal. My summer healing allowed me to reevaluate life and reflect. I spent a lot of time just sitting outside. I observed the birds and the trees, and I had realizations about the natural order of life.

I understood that no matter how fast or slow we decide to go as humans, in the pace of our daily lives, nature continues to go at its own pace. I began to understand that you cannot speed up nature and that it simply goes at the pace that it is meant to. Perhaps in my life I was doing too much or working too hard in an attempt to "get somewhere fast."

It was during this summer that Duggan presented his poem, "The Urgency of Rest," and asked me if I would be interested in illustrating it. I sat and read the poem in awe, realizing that the words of his poem perfectly described the epiphanies I had just so recently concluded about life.

In this very moment, I was reminded that even in this time of rest, my life continued to flourish. I couldn't sing, yet there I was being presented with an opportunity to reconnect with my visual art. My life continued to move at nature's pace even though I was not working tirelessly or seeking anything. This is the very idea of "The Urgency of Rest," and it seemed serendipitous that I was being asked to illustrate the concept.

After one drawing, Duggan asked me to illustrate more. A blessing in disguise, I was able to channel my time healing into the drawings that now represent the poems in this book.

Editor's note: *For more of Hilary's work, please visit*

www.hilarykuhlmey.com.

Colorist Christina Dietz

Christina's Color Story

I learned lessons of a lifetime from being sick and undiagnosed
in my early twenties, prompting me to miraculously crave color:
in fruits and veggies, creating colorful art, and being drawn
to vibrant countries like New Zealand, Bali, India, Mexico, and
the western coast of Australia. Later I found out my bizarre
intuitive color craving was my body and mind supporting
myself during my journey with mycotoxin poisoning, aka "black
mold" poisoning. While undiagnosed and unaware, I
instinctively used my intuition through color in a myriad of
practical ways to help heal myself emotionally, mentally,
spiritually, even physically.

Color Therapy Art: Juice for the Human Spirit

I create medicinal color therapy art to nourish and enliven our
spirits to carry us along the human journey. *I believe we are the
stars.* We are quite literally composed of light cells, and
everything we physically interact with in our world is light
energy. Through color, different wavelengths of light, we can
experience rich, loving, miraculous Oneness. We are so blessed
to be together. This light cell art is made by lighting colors on
fire over a clear glass panel. I am thankful to be a part of them
freely creating and transforming themselves right before my
eyes. In person, the art feels and looks alive. Divinely kissed.

Integrative Color Therapy Practice:
Mixing Psychology, Plants, Beauty, and Wisdom

I have an integrative color therapy practice in Austin where I see clients in my private studio. This is not art therapy, but rather a highly evolved, intuitive, self-directed system. Aura-Soma is originally from London, now most practiced in Japan and Australia, and still a new gem to the States. I am intensively trained to practice Aura-Soma, a natural, sensory, positive approach to therapy and personal development interacting with color frequency made from plants, flowers, and minerals.

First, clients choose everyday aromatherapy colors to apply and inhale to recharge at an emotional and mental level to warm up. Then, clients choose from a different branch of mineral- and plant-infused colors to receive their own transformative wisdom as we talk through each bottle, reflecting amazing insight for every person.

I also facilitate group work for team and community building at businesses and organizations and bring the colors into event spaces to facilitate positive energy and joy.

Editor's note: *For more of Christina's work, please visit:*

HeartArtColorTherapy.com

AdventuringinColor.com

Made in the USA
Columbia, SC
06 February 2019